Give Them What They Want

❦

Turning Sunday School Into A Place Where People Want To Be

Michael H. Clarensau
&
Clancy P. Hayes

GOSPEL PUBLISHING HOUSE
Springfield, MO 65802-1894
02-3148

Contents

Preface

A recurring question voiced by church leaders is "How can we increase the number of people we are impacting with the gospel?" You have probably asked that question yourself. This book is an attempt to answer this vital question.

The authors have identified eight felt needs that are common to all people regardless of age. The authors contend that when church ministries give people what they are looking for, people will respond with their attendance and their attention.

Giving people what they want doesn't have to compromise the gospel, but rather can further the purposes of the kingdom of God. The common needs of humanity are a reflection of God's design in each of us. It is the challenge to all of us involved in Christian education to work with God and His purposes as we labor to bring people into heightened levels of spiritual maturity.

The format of this book combines inspirational reading with instructional material. Each chapter is introduced by a story based on a scriptural account. Expanding the reality of the characters by suggesting what they may have thought or felt increases the connection of our experiences to theirs. Each chapter also provides an example of a local church that models the positive results that occur when the leadership of the church commit themselves to meeting people's needs in relevant ways.

This book is intended to address a variety of readers. Local pastors will benefit because it will acquaint them with the basic needs of the generation to whom they are ministering. The suggestions given can be applied to a wide range of ministries for which they are responsible. The challenge of focusing the ministries of the church on felt needs is primarily the responsibility of the pastor. Coming to grips with the importance of the message of this book is the first step in a long-term growth process.

If you teach Sunday School and want to be relevant to your students, this book will provide you with the tools to accomplish this goal. The Sunday School is still the most efficient way to assimilate people into the body of Christ. If people are not plugging into your Sunday School because they view it as an outdated program, it is your responsibility to help change that perspective. Applying the principles in this book will help you change your image.

Leaders in the other ministries of the church will also benefit from reading this book. The principles presented here apply to people in general. Those involved in children's ministries, youth ministries, and adult ministries will all find insights here that will help them disciple more people in a more effective manner.

A leader's manual is provided for those who would like to use this book in a group training session. The leader's manual furnishes discussion aids as well as worksheets that will be useful in break-out sessions. One of the challenges when developing a book like this is to provide specific help for each of the developmental stages of those with whom we work. The leader's manual helps to meet this challenge. Four age-level specialists have provided training pages in the leader's manual that will help teachers develop practices in their individual ministries that will meet those specific developmental needs.

A special thanks to Carey Huffman, Verda Rubottom, Sharon Ellard, and Rhonda Curtis for their assistance in the development of this book. Their insights and assistance were of great value throughout the conceptualization and development process.

1

They want friends.

"People long to be a part of a community that will care for them. . . . They are drawn in more often by the warmth of relationship than the brilliance of apologetics."

Rebecca Manley Pippert

The soup barely stirred as Aaron plunged a crust of bread into the bowl. With no meat and only a few dried vegetables, the potential for a tasty meal didn't exist. But it was all they had—all they would ever have.

The other men took their usual places around the fire, silently devouring their meal for this day. There was no need for conversation. Over the years, every man's sad story had been told, every thought shared, every disappointment described in full detail. No one spoke of the future, for the future held nothing for any of them—nothing but pale soup and dried bread.

Aaron had never imagined life as a leper. The second son of one of Manasseh's most prominent families, he had anticipated a life in business with his brothers. In just a few years, he had proven his abilities, bringing in even more money than his older brother. Those days seemed long ago now.

Aaron looked at the odd collection of men around the campfire. There were nearly a dozen of them now. The lives they once enjoyed would have never brought them to fellowship with one another—two farmers, a tax collector, a few businessmen, some born to privilege, others who knew nothing but begging, and a priest. Now they sat around the meager fire, united by the white, deteriorating flesh that had driven them from their homes.

Home. The thoughts still overwhelmed Aaron. The faces of his beautiful wife and young son were permanently carved in his heart. Rachel's rich, dark eyes had attracted him from the moment they met. Her beauty had consumed him, making every other part of life seem pale. Such hope they once had. Such dreams they had dreamed together. The birth of their son had been the glorious beginning of their lives. How he missed them, longed to hold them. Now only their eyes could hold each other. The evident barrier his disease had built would keep them apart forever.

Of course, it was a barrier none could penetrate. Aaron's eyes moved across the lonely bunch. Each man had family and friends too. But—not anymore. Their loneliness had brought them together, and together they had survived. But even their friendship was hollow. They were untouchable, even to one another.

Reuben, the old tax collector, stood suddenly and looked toward the horizon. "What is it, Reuben?" the priest asked, breaking the silence with the first words of the morning.

Reuben offered no response but began moving toward the group that had appeared over the hill.

"It's Jesus!" one of the beggars shouted.

Jesus! Aaron's heart nearly exploded. Every leper had heard of Jesus. Stories of His ability to heal the sick had been repeated along the border between Samaria and Galilee for many weeks. He had even healed lepers, or so the stories had said.

Though unable to run, something had stirred in each of them. They fought their way over the rough stones. "Jesus, have mercy on us!" Aaron heard himself scream. Then the air was filled with their cries.

Jesus stopped, and the group around Him turned to look at the lepers. The lepers stopped too, knowing instinctively the distance required by the law. The groups stood at the necessary distance from one another, separated by more than the stones between them.

Yet, even at a distance, Aaron could see something different, something special, in the eyes of the One called Jesus. "Go, show yourselves to the priests." Jesus' words penetrated the warm air of the morning.

Aaron looked at his feet. The deathly flesh still hung to his frail frame, but he didn't hesitate. The others were already clamoring over the rocks, heading toward the city. Aaron knew the wave of hope that had flooded him also swept through each of them.

That's when the shouts began. "Look!" Reuben was the first to cry out. The older man's eyes were wide and bright with joy as he turned and extended his arms for all to see. The flesh was pure, more perfect than the day of his birth. Reuben fell on his face, sobs shaking him. The other men watched in amazement, unaware for the moment that each of them had experienced the same healing.

But the moment ended quickly. Soon a celebration greater than that of a conquering army erupted among the rough stones. Men who hadn't been touched for years now embraced freely and danced about.

Aaron leaned against a rock, his eyes filled with the celebrations of the others. *Healed!* Tears formed streaks on his dusty face as he lifted one leg and then the other. It was over! The nightmare had ended—not in slow death as he had always imagined.

Rachel! Suddenly Aaron's thoughts were full of his family. After all this time . . . they would hold each other again. Before this day ended, he would hold his son in his arms. His heart could barely contain his excitement and eagerness.

"Come on!" the priest now urged. "What are we waiting for?" he exulted and broke into a joyous run toward the city. Each of them followed, suddenly able to maneuver over the rocks like young boys.

Aaron charged after them, imagining the moment he would burst into his home proclaiming the miracle Jesus had given him. But then he stopped. *Jesus.* Aaron watched as the others sped over the horizon. He would hold his family tonight, but there was something he had to do first.

Aaron turned back toward the rough rocks. Before day's end, he would be in the embrace of his family. First he would find Jesus.

Every dream he thought was lost now stood ahead of him, all because of Jesus. He would hold his family tonight, loved ones he had not been able to touch because of his leprosy. It was all his again . . . all because of Jesus.

*F*riends, who needs 'em?"

The frustrated spouting of a rejected teenager may feel right amid moments of turmoil, but the answer resounds even louder, "We all do!"

Ours is a culture at war with itself. We treasure independence in spite of our dependent nature. We applaud technologies that further isolate us from others, all the while dreaming of relationships that ultimately satisfy. We want self-sufficiency, but find loneliness intolerable. The independence we want and the dependence that we need stand at distant poles, out of reach of one another, creating a paradox for each of us.

We need friends. Our society has "outgrown" the close-knit family, but failed to outgrow its need of one. Largely gone are the days of multigenerational families under one roof. Our neighbors rarely meet us at the back fence. The faces of our coworkers change rapidly, the product of modern mobility in the workplace. Our home entertainment systems call us into social isolation as we experience the world from the comfort of our favorite chair. And the growth of technology allows us to study, visit garage sales, and even "attend" church without ever leaving the desktop.

We can work a mouse without outside contact, but are we really prepared to live this unsocial way? Most people aren't. Loneliness is rampant. As traditional sources for companionship fade, the hunger for lasting replacements emerges stronger than ever. Expectations of lasting relationships have crumbled. Aberrant and destructive relationships have emerged to fill some gaps. We need what we once had, but the trail of bread crumbs leading us back has been devoured by the vulture of our own individualism.

But all hope is not lost. In fact, the thirst for friendship is one your church was designed to quench.

Ask your students to give you reasons they attend your Sunday School class, and the answer most likely to land at the top of the list will have something to do with friends. In fact, in discovering why people came to church in the first place, you'll be hard-pressed to find a survey where the invitation by a friend or the need for friends isn't first on the list.

The Gospels overflow with stories of lonely, hurting people finding acceptance in the eyes of Jesus. Their physical maladies appear most obvious, but it was the healing of their loneliness that glued them to His band of disciples. He was offering the acceptance and love of God. There's a relationship you can count on!

It's not so different for you. As your class or group gathers each week, your students benefit from the content of your teaching. They're mindful of the spiritual growth becoming more evident in their thoughts and attitudes. They are appreciative of the snacks too. But it may be the relationships they're finding that drive their participation. After all, our need for God and our need for one another are at the root of our deepest longing.

This longing is common to all of us. We want friends.

MAKING IT HAPPEN

A quick survey of your Sunday School class or small group will likely reveal that a key reason your students attend is because of the friendships they've found in your group. And why not? The benefits of fellowship are of great importance in the body of Christ. We lean on each other, minister to one another, and build lives that are inter-twined with the lives of our fellow saints. Indeed, such deep rela-tionships are a key intent of our God in establishing His Church.

But how does it happen? More importantly, what can a teacher do to make sure it's happening effectively among the students? Churches are frequently described as friendly or unfriendly. While such tags may not always be applied accurately, they speak volumes about the potential for finding friends.

EMBRACE THE NEED

Before we tackle the practical aspects of making your class more friendship friendly, let's start with you, the teacher. We've already established that your students want and need friends. But are you prepared to facilitate such things? Many of the steps that make rela-tionships happen are dependent on the approach and attitude the teacher brings to the classroom.

1. Is your class student centered?

For decades the traditional model for learning in our culture could be described as teacher centered. Lecture was the primary method. Students sat in rows facing the podium, and the presentation skills of the teacher would make or break the learning experience.

The shift is toward student-centered learning, where a successful experience is defined by what the learner gains rather than merely by what the teacher says. In such an environment, the needs of the students drive the class more than the preferences of the teacher. While more will be said of this in the paragraphs that follow, it is essential that a teacher determine to be student centered if that means relationships will be facilitated.

2. Do you model friendship?

Good relationship-building classes are places where the teacher also finds relationships. If you don't find friends in your class, your students aren't likely to either. Even if you are teaching children several decades younger than you are, you can model friendship to your students by being a friend.

3. How's your staying power?

There is a strong connection between the relationship-building potential of a class and the stability of the teaching post. Students need stability in order to settle in and begin to open up to others. If they are uncertain of your commitment, they may be less likely to want to commit, both to the class and to their fellow students.

ENHANCE THE ENVIRONMENT

Once you've made your own commitment to make relationships happen in your class, there are some environmental issues to address. Consider these issues:

1. Does your classroom say "talk to me"?

The arrangement of your room says a lot about the possibility of finding friends. If your room is arranged with all chairs facing toward the teacher, you may be telling your students they should talk only to you. Chairs situated in a semicircle or around tables let your students know that you want them to talk to each other.

2. Do you expect interaction?

Varying your methods so students get involved with each other also communicates expectation. Students who talk to each other while learning are more likely to become friends than those who speak only after class.

3. Do you take time for fellowship?

A class that begins or ends with opportunities to get acquainted is the ticket here. Refreshments, or perhaps the use of background music, will get students talking to one another and create an environment where they will relax and take quality steps toward building friendships.

4. Is your class a safe place?

While this issue is critical in children's classes, people of all ages thrive in a safe environment. If your class is a place where every student is valued and treated with kindness, students will welcome relationships. Teach kindness, both in word and example. Protect your students from any unkind treatment by others. Even "teasing," can heighten students' sensitivity and make them more reluctant to trust teachers or classmates.

Classes that build friendships often succeed because of environment more than any other factor. But establishing that environment can take time. Be patient and maintain your focus on friendship. Soon even a place formerly viewed as unfriendly can succeed.

ESTABLISH THE STRATEGY

If you're going to succeed in making your classroom a place where students can find the friends they need, you must be intentional. The best successes rarely happen by accident. Intentional strategy has the best chance of yielding the results you want. While a full list of possible ideas to include in your strategy could almost be endless, consider adding a few of the following to your own thoughts.

1. Survey your status.

Do you want to know if yours is a friendly class? Ask your students. A candid discussion of the experiences and feelings that they remember from the first day they attended can open your eyes to how new students really feel. Who spoke to you? Who made you feel welcome? What could we have done better? Why did you come back? Candid answers and discussion of these questions can help the entire group be more effective in extending friendship to one another.

2. Encourage interaction.

It seems straightforward enough, but many students need a little push in the area of interaction. For children, you may want to encourage students to play or work together on a project. Teens are almost always game for a project or discussion. Even adults benefit from encouragement to talk to one another. If a student raises a question, why not let another student try to answer? Teaching methods that get students talking to each other open the way for friendships to be built and strengthened.

3. Learn about each other.

What do your students know about each other? Probably not as much as you think. Sharing fun facts about students with the rest of the class can open the way to get better acquainted. "Did you know Pat is a science teacher?" "Denise makes the best chili I've ever tasted!" "Dave and Pam spent a few years overseas." "Julie has a new puppy named Sparky." These little bits of biography may spark conversations that lead to friendship.

4. Respond to needs.

It is said that the deepest friendships are built in times of crisis. When students face times of difficulty, bring the class in to help. Expressions of love and friendship, such as providing food, offering a helping hand, and holding special times of prayer all bond your students closer together.

5. Share follow-up responsibilities.

Nowhere is it written that the teacher must shoulder the whole load. That's good news. One responsibility you can share is follow-up. Asking Dave to let Jeff know we missed him virtually guarantees a conversation between the two. And Jeff will be impressed. "Dave's not even the teacher, and he gave me a call!"

6. Plan friendship events.

Amid the fast pace of life, it is tempting to believe that your students are too busy for a party. But such events provide the best environment for finding friends. Be intentional in planning a fellowship event. Know why you're getting together and what you hope to see happen. Such intentionality will keep you on track and let you know when you've succeeded.

Once you start targeting these principles, you'll be amazed how easy it is to help your students find friends. And when they find their friends in your class or group, they'll need no other reason to attend and participate in the learning experiences you have prepared for them.

ENGAGE THE STUDENT

There are numerous ideas you can discover to help your students find friendship in your class. The key step is to start looking for them. When you make relationships a priority, they'll start happening. Your students want friends. Often you just have to facilitate the opportunities for friendship.

1. See the individual.

Never forget that you teach a group of individuals, not a herd of humans. Some of those individuals will need more help finding friends than others. Identify those students, and set a strategy to help them. Maybe they lack certain social skills or haven't had friendship modeled effectively. Perhaps they are a bit abrasive or reluctant to draw close to others. Helping such students may take more work, but it's worth the effort.

2. Be the first friend.

When a student needs a friend, the teacher is the best choice. You are the class leader, and the friendship you extend to an individual sets an example and expectation for the rest of the students. If you love the rowdy student who carelessly knocked down the walls of Jericho the group just completed, soon your students will extend forgiveness and be friends too.

3. Help each student contribute.

The ability to make friends is often directly connected to whether a person fits in with others. While some are naturally gregarious and need little help finding their place, others don't find comfort so easily. Finding a way for these students to contribute helps them feel they belong, and those are the feelings that open the way to relationships.

People want friends. In fact, it may be the most fundamental felt need in your church and community. If you can help people find in your classroom or church the friendship they're seeking, you will cement them to the ministry of your class and your church. After all, we all want to be where our friends are.

IT'S HAPPENING

Evangel Temple Christian Center located in Springfield, Missouri, has produced a Sunday School system that excels in fostering interpersonal relationships. This is especially true of the adult classes, but it is also true of the children and youth classes.

The adult Sunday School classes at Evangel Temple are designed to develop bonds that last a lifetime. Some classes have been together as a unit for almost as long as the thirty years the church has existed. During this time, students have walked through the stages of life together, learning from one another, celebrating the victories experienced, and crying together in times of tragedy. As class members make their way along the journey of life together, the relationships that are being built grow stronger and stronger.

The youth of Evangel Temple are also known for their deep friendships. They look forward to being together several times throughout the week. One manifestation of this is the weekly "snack and yak" after church each Sunday evening. Nearly the entire youth group makes their way to a local restaurant each week for this informal gathering. The youth pastor facilitates this by providing transportation for those too young to drive. Each Sunday evening at about nine o'clock the youth building parking lot at Evangel Temple fills with parents coming to pick up their young people who have participated in this relationship-building event. This also serves to strengthen relationships between parents who use the time to engage in additional fellowship themselves.

The children at Evangel Temple are encouraged to build strong relationships as well. This intentional approach occurs both in the children's church area and in the children's Sunday School classes. The architecture of Evangel Temple's Sunday School area is conducive to relationship building. The "pods" are open with no one sitting at a desk. Handwork is done sitting around community tables. But for much of the class students are encouraged to move around and participate with one another in a learning-center approach. Over the years this approach has helped teachers build lasting relationships with their students and with one another.

The relationships built through Sunday School at Evangel Temple do not occur by accident. The church intentionally uses its Sunday School classes as ministry units. When a death occurs within the family of a Sunday School class member, that class plays a major role in ministering to the family. Sunday School at this church provides care and fellowship in addition to instruction.

One of the keys for Evangel Temple's success in the area of relationship building is the time allotted to Sunday School. The schedule at Evangel Temple allows ninety minutes between the end of the first service and the beginning of the second service. This lengthy period of time provides ample opportunity for students to sit around, enjoy a snack, catch up on the week's happenings, and still engage in a lengthy interaction with the Scriptures.

A highlight of the Evangel Temple calendar is the annual all-church campout for all age levels in a family setting. This event begins on a Friday evening and goes through Sunday afternoon. It is designed to bring members of the church together in an informal setting to foster relationships. Each evening members of the church can be seen sitting around campfires eating smores, drinking coffee, and telling stories. These intimate scenes are a reflection of the relationships encouraged in the Sunday School classroom throughout the year.

The secret to Evangel Temple's success with building relationships is a result of its intentional approach. The leaders provide ample time in class to fellowship, plan events that promote informal interaction, and encourage class members to respond to the needs of those within their primary unit of contact. This approach is within the grasp of any church. Relationships are important. Follow Evangel Temple's example and create an atmosphere where relationships will grow.

A FINAL LOOK

Sounds of hatred, sarcasm, and blasphemy filled the air as Robert followed a prison guard on a tour of the state penitentiary. Tattooed men made crude gestures from behind the cold steel bars that constrained them. Not all the prisoners were aggressive toward Robert. Some sat in their cells, seemingly ignorant that a curious spectator had invaded their space.

As Robert walked down the hallways that separated the rows of cells, his mind was filled with images of what these men's lives could have been had they simply made different decisions in the past. Robert fought the urge to feel superior to those held in captivity as he walked freely among them. It would have been easy for him to feel proud of all the good choices he had made that had preserved his own freedom.

The moment Robert had looked forward to finally arrived. He was given the opportunity to interview a middle-aged convict named Claude. The result of that interview permanently changed the way he looked at himself and the way he viewed those who were serving time for criminal offenses.

Claude had not enjoyed an easy life by anybody's standards. While Claude was still a young boy, his father was tragically killed in a bar room brawl. His mother, left to provide for the family by herself, soon found it necessary to go back to work. She got a job in a diner waiting tables, but this did not pay her enough money to provide food and shelter for herself and her young son.

Soon Claude's mother was offered a job as a dancer at an exotic bar in town. She resisted at first, but she was eventually lured into accepting the offer as the need for money grew. Her new job meant long nights and poor associations. Claude was left home alone at night, watching television lonely and bored.

News of Claude's mom's new employment rapidly made its way through his town. Claude's friends no longer played with him because their parents feared the evil influence he would have on them. Those who once were Claude's best friends began to make fun of him and call him names.

Claude became increasingly lonely and bitter. He developed hatred toward his mother, toward himself, and toward everyone who had ever hurt him. He didn't understand why all of this had happened to him. All he wanted was to feel normal and to have friends.

As Claude grew older, he began wishing that his mother wouldn't come home. He devised plans to get back at her and eliminate the succession of men who emerged from her bedroom each morning. He didn't know how he would do it, but he knew that one day he would put an end to his shame and to the situation that entrapped him.

Claude began hanging around older boys who provided him alcohol and drugs in exchange for different kinds of favors. Being young and impressionable, he was an easy target for them. They would often send him into stores to steal things for them. But Claude didn't care. At least these guys talked to him and treated him like a person. They didn't make fun of him or bring up his mother's lifestyle. Claude looked forward to being with these guys. He would do anything he could to keep their favor. He began to feel that he had finally found a place where he was accepted.

On Claude's fourteenth birthday, things spiraled downward. He had stolen from stores so often that he thought nothing of robbing a local liquor store. He casually walked up to the counter, pulled a knife, and demanded that the clerk give him all the money that was in the cash register. Claude got about five hundred dollars and a couple of bottles of rum. He didn't realize that the clerk had sounded an alarm and that his image was caught on the store's surveillance cameras. Soon the police had Claude in custody. At the young age of fourteen, Claude experienced the prison system firsthand.

Claude spent two years in detention for that crime. When he was released at age sixteen, he went back to his mother's home. A much older, much more used woman greeted him. After about a week, his mother told him that she couldn't afford to let him live with her. So Claude turned and walked out of his mother's house for the last time. He had no place to go, no one to turn to except for the old gang.

Claude's old friends welcomed him gladly. They wanted to hear all about his prison time. Claude quickly became a part of the group, participating once again in the drugs, alcohol, and crime.

One fateful night, Claude and three of his friends decided to rob a convenience store. Things got out of hand. Claude shot and killed the clerk. Later, Claude's friends testified against him. Sadly, within months of his release from custody, Claude was again sitting in prison, only this time he was waiting to be tried as an adult.

Claude almost cried as he recalled the moment when the judge gave him a life sentence for his cold-blooded crime. Fortunately for Claude, the death penalty had been suspended in his state. Claude didn't know if or when he would get out of prison, but in some ways it didn't matter because prison had become his home, and his fellow prisoners had become his family.

Robert's conversation with Claude brought about a change in his perspective toward the men and women who are in prison. No longer did he feel superior to them. Instead, he became thankful for the acceptance he had found in his family, in the church he attended, and in the friends he had. Robert wondered where he would be if he had experienced the type of rejection that Claude had known.

Robert's encounter with Claude made him see how essential it is for people to find acceptance and how important it is for those in healthy relationships to offer acceptance to those who need it.

2

They want a sense of purpose.

"Few men ever drop dead from overwork, but many quietly curl up and die because of under-satisfaction."

Sydney Harris

John smiled and shook his head as he listened to his brother, James, talking . . . talking . . . talking. He had known his news would excite his brother. James was easily excited. John knew he'd spend the entire morning nodding while his brother talked.

That's why he had waited until they were alone on the fishing boat before telling James about the one he'd met. He didn't want his father in earshot of James' reaction. Dad didn't care much for his sons' ideas of greater things. The fishing business had been enough for him, and he offered a constant reminder that, if they were smart, it would be enough for them too.

John knew fishing would never be enough for James. It seemed he'd been hearing James' grand dreams all of his life. "I'm going to do something important," James had said a hundred times. Although his brother's dreams hadn't progressed much, John was convinced that James would ultimately find a different life. *Deep down, Father knows it too.* John was convinced of that as well.

John rarely argued the point with his father. James had done enough arguing for both of them. Besides, fishing wasn't a bad life, and John hated to see his parents' hurt expressions when the subject of the family business came up. Barring some unforeseen event, John knew he'd end up with the fishing business and help care for his parents in their old age.

Still James babbled on. Simon and Andrew were just across the inlet, but their proximity didn't concern John. They had heard James' ideas before. They seemed to feel the same as John did.

At least Andrew did. Simon was more stubborn. He didn't care much for the wild dreams James spouted, and the talk of Messiah's coming was even less sensible to him. John had memorized Simon's hearty laugh at the thought that any of them would ever see the Messiah.

But Andrew believed. He wasn't as boisterous about it as James was, but Andrew definitely believed. He was a man of action. It was Andrew who had brought word of the Baptist to their fishing circle. James and John had gone with him to hear the wilderness preacher many times, often enough to be considered among his followers, but none had followed the Baptist more closely than Andrew.

Simon had shown some interest, but he usually stayed behind with the nets, trying to keep their family's business afloat. Simon was the best fisherman among them. He seemed content with that accomplishment.

But that was before today. Things were less animated in the other boat, but John knew Andrew had told his brother the same story that he'd shared with James. Simon seemed to be processing the news slowly, while James had launched into an endless oration on it. That was expected of James. John smiled and wondered if Andrew was smiling too.

It *was* incredible news. John could hardly blame James for his excitement. In fact, yesterday's events made John want to do some talking too. He and Andrew had spent most of the morning searching for the Baptist. They found him in a favorite spot near the Jordan. James had promised Father he wouldn't leave the nets for a few days, needing to prove to the old man that he would shoulder his share of responsibility. But his moment of dedication had been costly.

As John and Andrew approached those gathered around the Baptist, they noticed their mentor seemed distracted, gazing off into the wilderness, seemingly oblivious to the barrage of questions being hurled his way. That's when they saw Him. He wasn't a large man, and His garment was simple, but something about Him had captured the full attention of the wilderness preacher.

"Behold, the Lamb of God who takes away the sin of the world!" The Baptist's proclamation stunned the entire group.

"You mean . . . you mean?" Andrew stuttered the question.

The Baptist offered no response. He kept his gaze on the man moving across the desert. For weeks they had heard their mentor speak of the one who was to come. Was this He? Andrew broke into a run, but soon John overtook him as they led a small band of the curious.

When they approached, the man most knew as Jesus, the Baptist's cousin, turned to greet them. "What do you want?" He asked. John remembered thinking the answer to such a question could take all day.

They had spent the rest of the day with Him. By the time Andrew and John returned home that night, their brothers had gone to bed. Hardly able to contain their excitement, they had turned in as well. Morning always came early for fishermen.

Now the news was out. James was proclaiming the news of the Messiah to any fish that would listen. "There's more to life than fishing, John," he offered with passion. John nodded, eager to share his own thoughts, but reluctant to interrupt his brother's dissertation.

Soon Andrew and Simon had moved their boat alongside, and the four men devoured their lunches along with talk of the Lamb of God. Even Peter was excited. What would this mean for Israel? Had God really chosen this moment to fulfill their greatest hope? Had news reached the synagogue? There was so much to discuss, so much to debate, so much to be fulfilled.

In the middle of their excited discussion, a voice called to them from the shore.

"It's Him," Andrew almost shouted. Immediately James was on his feet, waving frantically.

"James, control yourself," John urged. "You're rocking the boat!"

Simon and Andrew laughed. There was no calming their impetuous friend.

Jesus stood on the shore as they rowed the boats toward Him. Peter and Andrew arrived first, despite James' frantic paddling. "Come, follow me," Jesus broke the silence, "and I will make you fishers of men."

Simon and Andrew didn't hesitate. They barely tethered the boat to shore before clamoring after Him.

Immediately Jesus turned His attention toward the second boat. But the two sons of Zebedee needed no further invitation. James nearly crushed his brother as he climbed over him. But John didn't hesitate either.

Jesus smiled and turned back toward the village. The four fishermen followed His confident strides, unconcerned for the boats and nets and father left behind.

"I told you there's more to life than fishing," James chattered as they hurried to catch up to Jesus.

*D*o you want to make a difference? Most of us do. The need to be significant often motivates the heart of most adults. We want to know that we matter.

Childhood and adolescence are dominated by our need for security, identity, and acceptance. Those needs play a role in adult life as well. But with maturity comes the acknowledgement of mortality and the growing desire to know that our lives matter. We want our opinions to be heard, our values preserved, our mark deeply carved into the fabric of our world. We are no longer content with a will that merely disburses our assets at life's end. Now we want to leave a legacy, giving evidence to future generations of our significance.

This hunger for meaning drives our choices. Many jump from job to job to pursue career goals. For most the idea of spending forty years with the same company seems unlikely and even unhealthy. We no longer attend church out of mere loyalty or habit either. We want meaning and value in exchange for our time. In response, the church has opted to speak in terms such as "purpose driven" and "vision casting" to meet the demand for more meaning.

Of course, there are numerous purposes to choose from. Much of our world needs saving. Whales, beaches, and rainforests only start the seemingly endless list of the endangered. Causes present themselves on the moral front as well. Feeding the hungry, protecting the unborn, guarding the rights of the elderly, and opposing genocidal conflicts are just a few of the options. Community involvement looks for participants as well, offering purpose and meaning in civic duty. The escalation of the call for mentors encourages us to find fulfillment by influencing young lives.

Despite this wealth of opportunity, people are still looking for purpose. Recent findings of the Barna Research Group reveal that "an astounding proportion of adults—43%—admit that they are 'still trying to figure out the meaning and purpose of my life.'" And it's no surprise that this is a keen question among Baby Busters, our younger adults, where 56 percent are still looking for meaning and purpose.[1]

Where do you find purpose? If you're reading this book, you've likely been exposed to or already discovered the remarkable purpose of serving Jesus Christ. You see, His purposes are eternal. The pursuit of God and the fulfillment of His will in our churches, communities, and world offer the highest purpose humanity can achieve. When Jesus turned a group of fishermen into fishers of men, He launched them into a destiny filled with incredible challenge, but even greater meaning. That's the purpose He extends to you and to every student who enters your classroom.

In fact, that purpose is extended to every child, every teen, and every adult in your community. They want purpose—we've got purpose. It's a perfect match.

MAKING IT HAPPEN

When people feel they have a purpose in life, they can make it through the mundane that occupies much of their existence. Those who feel they are simply taking up space in this world often fall into despondency and despair. The Bible makes it clear that God has a design and purpose for each person He has created. It is the responsibility of the Church to help people identify their gifts and talents and devise ways to become fully functioning members of their communities. Here is a plan designed to help students develop a sense of purpose.

EMBRACE THE NEED

As an active participant in your church, you may find it difficult to believe that some people can feel they have little purpose in life. You probably feel overwhelmed at points with the degree of responsibility that you have been given. Here are some concepts that will help you embrace this real need.

1. Everyone has a unique place in the kingdom of God.

A key principle of Scripture is that the Church is complete only when all its members are functioning together in harmony. A basic presupposition is that all Christians have at least one gift God has given to them that they are expected to contribute to the ministry mix of their church. If people fail to exercise that gift, or no room is given for that gift to function, the church will suffer.

When teachers understand this premise, they will look for ways to raise expectations of their students, encourage students to develop their gifts, and devise ministry opportunities where these gifts can be explored. Teachers who monopolize the ministry opportunities in their classrooms exhaust themselves and limit the potential of students of all ages.

2. God's purposes are the ultimate expression of one's humanity.

Each of us has been created first and foremost to be in relationship with God and to fulfill His purposes. To attempt to find meaning outside of service to God is pointless. Although some non-

Christians may find temporary satisfaction through benevolent acts or fame, (in the long run they will be left to search elsewhere to find what they are looking for.) As a teacher of God's Word, you can offer people the opportunity to discover who they are in Christ and help them fulfill their ultimate destiny through service to God and to their fellow human beings. Keeping this in focus will help you maintain a balance between the communication and cultivation aspects of your ministry.

3. People need help in finding purpose and significance.

As you look around your church or classroom, take note of the students who seem to feel good about themselves and those who demonstrate a lack of self-confidence. Generally you will discover that it is the student who is actively involved who shows confidence. Teachers must understand that the students who sit back and fail to get involved do not necessarily like being in that condition. If asked, most would say that they would like to be confident participants in their community. Unfortunately, they often don't know how to move from being onlookers to integral members of the group.

ENHANCE THE ENVIRONMENT

Once you have recognized the need for helping your students discover a sense of purpose, it is important to create class dynamics to help make that a reality. Here are a few ideas to move you toward accomplishing that goal.

1. Believe in people.

Your students are able to sense if you have confidence in them and their ability to minister. If you go behind them, fixing their mistakes, students will quickly quit trying and allow you to resume ownership for the entire ministry. People will fail from time to time as they attempt to grow in their ministry. Be available to coach them, but avoid the temptation to do their ministry for them. As you show confidence in them, they will become more adept at what they do and will feel a sense of accomplishment.

2. Cultivate dreams.

Don't limit people by your dreams. Allow students to think beyond the typical ministry opportunities traditionally engaged in by members of your church. Challenge students to seek God for what He would have them do with the gifts and talents He has assigned them. Be willing to allow your students to experiment with the dreams they have been given. Make your classroom an accepting place where students can fine-tune start-up ministries.

3. Set high expectations.

No student in your classroom should be allowed to simply sit and soak. Those students who are not participating in ministry, using their God-given gifts to serve others in the ways they can, are not fulfilling God's plan for their lives. Continually remind your class members that God has a plan and purpose for their lives. Inform your students that it is your responsibility to encourage them to reach their potential usefulness to God and His kingdom.

ESTABLISH THE STRATEGY

Every church needs an intentional, well-planned system of mobilizing and supporting the giftedness of its members. Here are a few elements to include as you develop a system that will work for your individual situation.

1. Help people understand who they are in Christ.

One thing that keeps people from feeling a sense of purpose is a previously developed sense of worthlessness. Sadly, many people develop a negative self-worth early in life. Divorce, abuse, addiction in the home, and inconsiderate teachers leave children feeling that they are worth less than other children who come from better environments. This feeling of worthlessness carries over into adulthood for many. Unfortunately, these feelings don't immediately go away when a person becomes a Christian. It is your responsibility to remind these individuals that they are loved and valued by Jesus. Help students to understand that, as painful as the past may be, they can trade the damning conditions that bound them in the past for freedom available to them through their relationship with Christ.

2. Help people discover their gifts.

Once you have helped students realize that they have great potential in Christ, it is your privilege to help them discover their gifts and talents. There are many spiritual gift inventories that will help you guide your students in this discovery process. An excellent resource you can use to help with this entire process is a book titled *Getting Into The Game*, edited by Larry Thomas and published by Gospel Publishing House. This book is designed to help leaders identify potential in people and to plug them into appropriate ministries.

It is important to remember that the gifts and talents people possess are not all supernatural in nature. The Bible reveals that there are gifts of healings, but there are also gifts of helps and hospitality. Treat all gifts equally and encourage students to be open to use every gift and ability God has given to them for His glory.

3. Help people become purpose driven.

People who are purpose driven know what God wants them to do and find fulfillment as they accomplish the ministry they have been called to. Those who stay on task will avoid the wandering feeling that is typical of those who feel worthless. It will also help to eliminate the competition that occasionally will arise in churches when people begin to engage in ministries for which they have no calling or equipping.

4. Help prepare people to act.

Not all learning comes through the transference of facts and figures. Often teachers must use a hands-on approach that assists students to gain knowledge of the ministries God has called them to. It is likely that you do not possess all of the ministry gifts represented in your classroom, yet you will be called on to help equip people for service. Be wise in selecting other people in the church who can mentor those who are beginning in a ministry for which you lack skills. Be especially careful that the mentors you select are encouragers who will build up the people with whom they work.

ENGAGE THE STUDENT

Some of your students will be hesitant to get involved in ministry. They will have a hard time overcoming the negative baggage that has attached itself to them. Here are suggestions that will help you engage your students.

1. Find places of ministry.

As an influential person in the church, you have the keys that can open doors of ministry for those in your class. Help your students identify ministry opportunities that are available inside the local assembly as well as those in the community. Speak with other leaders, and recommend students who have potential to minister in their area of responsibility. If you teach children, find ways to involve them as helpers in your classroom. Everyone can find a place to help. Do whatever you can to prepare the way for each student.

2. Provoke involvement.

Keep before your students the importance of involvement in ministry. Use stories of those who have taken the risk of engaging in ministry and benefited themselves and the kingdom of God as a result. Each time a project in the church comes up that needs a task done that one of your students is equipped for, bring it to the attention of the student and the person in charge of the project.

3. Highlight successes.

Give attention to the success of your students' attempts of fulfilling God's purposes in their lives. Have students share how being involved in ministry has changed their lives. Ask your pastor to allow you to write an article about your students and their ministry involvement.

One of the most vital things you do as a teacher is to help others grow and develop in their ministry to God. In doing so, you help the individual feel fulfilled and you cooperate with God's plan for the church. So don't be content to let people in your class sit back and watch you minister week after week. Make it a point to engage them in ministry for the benefit of all involved.

IT'S HAPPENING

Faith Assembly of Lacey located in Lacey, Washington, has developed an approach to ministry that highlights the importance of having a sense of purpose, both individually and in the overall plan of the church. Dixie Zahn, Children's Pastor at the church, shared the philosophy of Faith Assembly of Lacey and some of the practical results associated with this purposeful approach.

The leadership of Faith Assembly of Lacey feels that the church is the ideal place for people to find a sense of purpose for their lives because the highest purpose for all people is to love God and obey His commands. If this purpose is not being accomplished in the Christian's life, the result will be aimlessness and lack of personal fulfillment. Pastor Zahn feels that "through the ministry of Sunday School, we have a unique opportunity to endeavor to fulfill the Great Commission by establishing clear purposes and measurable goals to see that we are accomplishing what God has asked of us." It is the goal of those who lead the Christian education ministry at Faith Assembly of Lacey to have teachers who not only tell Bible stories for informational purposes, but who also teach with the goal of helping people find purpose in their lives and who challenge students to live the gospel that they learn.

People who attend Faith Assembly of Lacey have an opportunity to find purpose through the five primary ministry areas offered by the church.

Those involved in the worship ministry feel a part of the overall ministry of the church as they use their musical gifts to touch the lives of those inside the sanctuary and minister to the greater Lacey community through outreach efforts.

The discipleship effort provides opportunities to find purpose for all age groups. Adults are discipled through Bible studies, Sunday School classes, and small group training sessions. Youth are discipled through missions trips, Saturday evening small groups, camps, Sunday School, and youth meetings. Children are viewed not only as the church of tomorrow but also as part of the church today. Children are trained to minister through music and drama and are instructed in methodology to become actively involved in the classroom experience. At all levels, the focus of the discipleship emphasis is to help people find purpose by becoming involved in meeting the needs of others.

The fellowship emphasis of the church helps people find a sense of purpose as they take time to get to know one another, to bear one another's burdens, and to share in each other's joys. Through fellowship people see themselves as valuable components of the local church and as contributors to the lives of others.

Evangelism at Faith Assembly of Lacey is expressed in many traditional and non-traditional ways. It is the goal of the leaders of Faith Assembly of Lacey to get people actively involved in the transformation process of salvation. People who discover their role in the Great Commission find fulfillment and direction for their own lives.

The fifth area of emphasis at Faith Assembly of Lacey is service. Service opportunities are provided in almost every ministry area of the church. People at Faith Assembly of Lacey are encouraged to take the Network Class to help them find their gifts and passions in ministry and to assume a place of ministry.

Pastor Zahn identified a young single mother who typifies the results of helping people find a sense of purpose. This young mother was struggling with life when she found faith and hope in the Lord through an evangelism outreach of Faith Assembly of Lacey. She and her children began attending the church and became involved in its ministries and steadily grew in their faith. This mother is now involved in ministry to young children. Recently she expressed the great joy she experienced when she prayed with a child to receive Christ for the first time. She has been transformed from an individual with little hope to one who now offers hope to others.

When asked what she would suggest for other churches that wanted to foster a sense of purpose, Pastor Zahn has this reply. "Take time to establish a sense of mission and purpose. You must take aim for something to reach the goal. Ministry is too critical to do in a haphazard manner." The leaders of Faith Assembly of Lacey have taken aim to establish a sense of purpose in those they minister to and with. The results are seen both in the lives of those who have found hope and in the lives of those who are actively offering it.

Bill stared aimlessly as the machine he maintained spewed its contents into rows of gleaming cans before him. The endless rows of cans traveling slowly along the conveyer belt seemed to represent the monotony of Bill's life. Day after day he stood in the same spot, saw the same sights, and heard the same rhythmic sound of the machines that surrounded him. The only relief from his mundane existence was when his machine would break down and require repairs. It seemed ironic that trouble with the machinery became the highlight of Bill's day.

Bill often dreamed of another life in another place. It wasn't that he didn't like living with his wife of twenty-five years. And he had a pretty good relationship with his three nearly grown children. Money was not the problem either. Working in the cannery for over two decades had been very good to him financially. Three cars, a five-bedroom home, and a spa in the backyard attested to his monetary success. Most people looked at Bill and wished they could have a life as good as his. But all of these "things" brought very little satisfaction to Bill.

As the cans continued to make their way past him, Bill wondered about the impact he was having on others. Sure he was providing for his family, but in many ways he felt more like an ATM machine than he did a human being. He kept the money machine filled so others could satisfy their desires. But recently he realized that each time he filled the machine with crisp bills reaped from his tedious hours of labor, he felt increasingly empty.

At first Bill was happy with his life. He would work all week at the factory and then party with his family all weekend. Gathering his wife and young children in the family van for a weekend at the lake was exhilarating for Bill. But after a while, neither he nor his family looked forward to these previously anticipated weekend outings. As the kids grew, they decided that time with their friends was more important than time with Mom and Dad. Although this attitude hurt Bill, he could understand because he had been there as a teen himself. Bill sought other ways to find fulfillment. None of his attempts provided the long-lasting results he sought.

Bill hoped he was simply going through a phase and that he would get over the feelings of emptiness. He had heard that people sometimes feel like this when they hit the mid-life years. But as he looked around himself, he noticed other men his age who seemed fulfilled. For example, there was Jim who had stood just a few feet from him working on a similar machine for the last fifteen years. Bill didn't know what was wrong with him, but he did know he was sick of living without a purpose.

Jim smiled as he watched another can wind its way toward its final destination. He wondered where the can of creamed corn would eventually be consumed. He thought about the various places in the world that his company sold their product line. It was likely that one can would be opened by a wealthy family in the suburbs, while the contents of another can that traveled on the conveyer belt before him would find its way onto the plate of a child living in the ghetto. Jim was happy to be a part of the process that provided needed nutrients to so many different kinds of people.

Jim had not always been so excited about his job. For a long time, he had viewed his job as simply a place to make money. He could hardly wait to take his lunch pail and walk past the security officer on his way out of the building each day. Like Bill, Jim saw money as a tool to make himself and his family members happy.

But that all changed one day as Jim's Sunday School teacher was explaining a passage of Scripture from the Gospels. He had read the passage many times before, but this time he saw it in a new light. He discovered through this presentation that satisfaction isn't as much a result of what a person possesses as it is a result of what a person gives away. In other words, satisfaction is a result of shifting one's focus from "me" to "you."

This truth gripped Jim and caused him to rethink his priorities. When his pastor challenged him to go with his church on a mission trip, Jim's initial reaction was that he couldn't afford to spend his limited vacation time in such a manner. After a period of reflection, he realized that God was calling him to make the personal sacrifice. He went on the trip, and it changed his life further.

After that, Jim became involved in several outreach opportunities in his community. Now, he teaches a Sunday School class, serves meals to the poor at the local mission, and even cares for children in the church nursery.

When Bill decided to ask Jim why he seemed so happy, Jim told him that his satisfaction came from a sense of purpose he discovered when he started looking beyond his own situation. He pointed to the can that passed before them and explained how he used to think of it as a meaningless item of food. Since he had gone to the ghetto of a large city in Central America and seen the joy that a can of food brought to the children there, his perspective changed. Now each time a can passed by him, he saw the faces of children who needed someone to do work like his.

Bill walked away from his conversation with Jim wondering if he had just received the answer he had been looking for. Jim seemed to have found a purpose for living. He was eager to talk to Jim again. Maybe he could attend Sunday School with Jim and discover a sense of purpose as well.

ENDNOTE

[1]Barna Research Group, Ltd. (1997). *Angels are in—devil and Holy Spirit are out,* [Online]. Available FTP: www.barna.org

3

They want to have fun.

"If you have no joy, there's a leak in your Christianity somewhere."

Billy Sunday

Another business deal, another load of cash, another investment that would pay off for years. Soon he'd again be the buzz of the community. The prodigy does it again!

But all he could muster was a yawn. Success had become all too familiar in his life.

Future generations would know him simply as the rich young ruler. It was an appropriate title, for he was, indeed, all three. "Rich" had become almost an understatement. With his knack for mastering the economy, he had taken his father's small operation and constructed one of the most successful businesses in the entire region east of the Jordan. He was known for miles as a fair man, one whom God had obviously blessed.

"Young" was still an accurate description too. Though tall and stately in his manner, his youthful face and tender heart had earned him the label "boy wonder." Actually, his uncle had first tagged him with the nickname, but it stuck easily. Even as a child, he had shown ambition and leadership, always the organizer and strategist among his young friends. "He's always had the knack," his father frequently bragged.

Over the last few months, the "ruler" tag was becoming increasingly accurate too. His holdings were expanding faster than Joshua's ancient march across Canaan. He had purchased dozens of estates, promising to make a success of other families' inherited lands for only a small portion of the profits. Many people had trusted him. And why not? The region had never been more prosperous.

He was, indeed, a rich young ruler. And while his youth would ultimately slip from him, it seemed clear that the other two aspects of his identity would continue to increase.

He folded the transaction papers into his satchel and headed toward his office. How pleased his father and uncle would be to see the contracts. Likely the rest of the day would be spent in cele-bration—a big meal and plenty of toasts to the "boy wonder."

Yes, it had become all too familiar. Somehow, it just wasn't enough anymore. He shook his head, chiding himself for his fool-ishness. He was the envy of hundreds, maybe thousands. Who wouldn't want what he had? He knew many men who would wor-ship just about any god that would promise to give them abilities like his—to accumulate all the money he wanted, more than he could ever use. There were probably even more women who would trade places with his wife in a heartbeat. The jewelry, extrav-agant clothing from foreign lands, and a life of luxury had given her the look of a goddess. How could it not be enough?

At first, it had all been quite intoxicating. The money flowed faster than they could spend it. And the popularity . . . well, it's pretty heady stuff to be the talk of the town. The descriptions of his exploits had continued to grow, bringing the affirmation and respect of everyone he met. How could he not be happy?

But he wasn't. Life had lost its fun. He couldn't remember the last time he'd simply enjoyed a day. Laughter had become a rare experience too. The responsibilities he'd undertaken and the expectations others had thrust on him had stolen the joy he saw in others. Was this all there was? The words of Solomon, his hero since childhood, rang in his ears daily, "Meaningless! Everything is meaningless!"

He wanted to run in a field and not care whose field it was. He wanted to skip rocks across the Jordan and not be interrupted by someone needing investment advice. He longed to laugh at some silly happening until he could laugh no more. But there had been no reason to laugh for most of his life. *Why can't all this money buy what I want?* he wanted to yell at the skies.

His estate loomed on the horizon, but he secretly longed for somewhere else to go. At that moment, a crowd coming up the road stole his attention. Rumors had been flying since dawn that Jesus of Nazareth, the famous purveyor of eternal life, was in the area. *Must be Him*, he almost whispered.

The buzz hadn't interested him much. This miracle worker was the property of the poor. Few of the unhappy man's friends had shown much interest. "Those who have nothing will latch onto about anything," his uncle had said. He remembered nodding his agreement and dismissing the excitement in favor of more important things.

But he was having trouble dismissing it now. He had never expected such a scene. The man at the center of attention, presumably Jesus, was surrounded by a celebration. People were dancing! Men and women seemed to be exploding with joy and laughter. And the children . . . the children couldn't resist the parade. They took turns jumping into Jesus' arms, climbing onto His back, beaming with excitement.

Suddenly, their lack of possessions seemed unimportant. They had something he wanted . . . badly. He could buy and sell the entire group, maybe even Jesus himself. And yet, the poorest among them seemed to have something his money couldn't buy.

The rich young man turned toward home, but his heart wouldn't let him leave. How much longer could he live like this? Was this a chance for real happiness? Home offered nothing but the piles of money he had become bored with. It just wasn't enough anymore.

At that moment, the child atop Jesus' shoulders caught his eye. The exhilaration in the young face sparked a jealousy in the man that he just couldn't contain. How he longed to trade places with the child, any child who possessed the joy he'd never found. He could resist no longer. The "boy wonder" wanted the wonder that young boy had.

Parting the crowd at a dead run, the rich young ruler bowed at the feet of Jesus, stopping the procession, but not the celebration. "Good teacher," he pleaded, "what must I do to inherit eternal life?"

*J*n America, we work hard and we play hard. At least that is the perception we have of ourselves. While there are many nations around the globe that have yet to whittle the workweek to our typical five days, our stress levels tell us we work hard.

And we want our time to play.

It has become our expectation that life be filled with fun. Simply put, we insist that life is to be enjoyed, and we have come to expect enjoyment in the things we do. We even want our work to be enjoyable!

Entertainment is a staple of our culture. In fact, it is one of our greatest priorities. And, we are willing to pay dearly for it. Athletes, actors, and the geniuses behind the entertainment industries are the most prevalent figures on the list of the wealthy. It is these that we treasure, for they are key sources of the fun we want and need.

Should such a focus on enjoyment drive our culture? One could argue that our imbalance in this area is ultimately unhealthy. But it's a philosophical argument that likely will have little impact on the practical realities surrounding us. The fact remains—people expect the activities that fill their leisure time to be enjoyable.

And that's the expectation people bring with them on Sunday

mornings or whenever the local church opens its doors to them. A blend of meaning and enjoyment is anticipated. If either is lacking, participation may be brief.

But there's more to the demand for fun than the cultural implications. Enjoyment is a powerful tool to motivate learning. Frankly, a bored learner is often not a learner at all. But add some fun to the mix, and you engage the individual on a deeper level. Fun brings enthusiasm, and regular participation and learning is an obvious by-product. We want to have fun, and we want to do the things that bring fun to our lives.

Should Bible truth be fun? Some would argue that the gravity of eternal truth supercedes the human need for enjoyment. There is no question that the power and importance of God's truth should never be lost amid fun and games. But, neither is a relationship with God void of enjoyment. The little band following Jesus around the Judean hillside hardly gives evidence of stoic staleness. Following Christ isn't a ticket to boredom. Those who follow Christ know it's fun to be a Christian!

The joy and enjoyment of life with Christ should reflect in every part of the local church's ministry. Every child, every teen, and every adult should find life to the fullest in their relationship with God. There's no denying the times of challenge a Christian will experience, but God's joy is built to penetrate even those hours of hardship.

People want enjoyment. In fact, many believe they are entitled to enjoyment. It's with that expectation that they will walk through your door. So let's show them how to really have fun!

MAKING IT HAPPEN

A speaker reflecting on his experience as a child involved in family devotions described those times with one word—*boring*. He attended the family gatherings not because he wanted to but because it was not optional. When he became an adult, he pledged that he would rather have no devotional time as a family than have a devotional time that his children would dread.

Your family devotion experience may have been similar to that speaker's. Unfortunately, the relationship between boring and the Bible have not been limited to times of family devotions. Church services and Sunday School classes have occasionally fostered this relationship as well. As a result, many adults who attended church and Sunday School as children refuse to do so as adults. As teachers, it is our responsibility to make church a place where people want to come and learn about our living and exciting Lord.

EMBRACE THE NEED

The teacher sets the tone of a classroom. If teachers desire to make Sunday School a place where people want to attend, they must plan for fun activities and view the classroom as a fun place to be. Sunday School can become the highlight of the students' week if you will determine to make it so.

1. Believe that enjoyment is a valid goal of the church.

It would be nice if Christians were intrinsically driven to pursue biblical knowledge regardless of the quality of the delivery system. The truth is that people today come to church when they see a benefit there for them that outweighs the benefit of going someplace else. Working with that reality we must also understand that no matter how good the information is that is being transmitted in the classroom, if people don't attend our churches and Sunday Schools, they will not benefit from our discipleship efforts. Providing fun and enjoyment is one way to draw people into the churches.

2. Understand that laughter and learning can go together.

For years Bill Cosby has made the world laugh. In the process he has taught us a great deal about ourselves. People all over the world set aside blocks of time weekly to hear his story and learn while they laugh. Christian comedians successfully use humor in communicating God's truth. While it is not suggested that the Sunday School teacher become a comedian, there is room for puns, jokes, and stories that tickle the funny bone while communicating the Word of God. Teaching the Bible is a serious endeavor, but it is possible to have fun and show reverence for God at the same time.

3. Make a commitment to be creative.

Doing things the way they have always been done will eventually become boring no matter how good it was in the beginning. Think about your favorite food or dessert. Now think about eating it every day for every meal for a month. Before long you would grow tired of it. The same is true in your classroom. If students can anticipate what they are going to experience week after week, they will soon find excuses not to be there or to cause disruption when they do attend. Teachers of successful classrooms understand that variety and creativity are vital for all age groups.

4. Realize that God is interested in our social concerns.

Some church leaders would like to focus just on the spiritual development of a person and leave the physical and social side to others. This approach to ministry stands in opposition to the mandates of Scripture. The Bible plainly teaches the importance of Christian community. God wants us to grow and develop spiritually, but He insists that we do so in the context of the body of Christ. The Bible is clear that God is concerned about the way we get along and enjoy one another. It is important to keep the whole person in mind as you prepare to teach God's Word.

ENHANCE THE ENVIRONMENT

As mentioned, the tone of the class is dependent on the teacher's initiation. Here are some ways that you can make the environment more conducive to enjoyment.

1. Have treats and snacks available.

It is not important that you supply the coffee/drinks and donuts/crackers each week, but it is your responsibility to see that it gets done. This could be through personal assignment or delegating the task of recruiting people to help. Refreshments are always a good way to make people feel comfortable and to set a friendly tone for the rest of the session.

2. Provide a time for personal interaction.

One reason people come to Sunday School and church is to see their friends. You can assess the social health of a church by the number of people who hang around after service and talk with one another. Since most Sunday School classes are immediately followed by the morning worship time, it is important to provide time before the class session if you want to foster personal interaction.

3. Keep things moving.

One of the enemies of enjoyment is stagnation. Asking people to stay in one place and listen to you will not bring a sense of fun regardless of the age of your students. When this is the case, the highlight of the class may become the dismissal prayer. Plan for a variety of activities each week.

4. Enhance the physical surroundings.

Posters, pictures, furniture, and toys for the younger children are just a few ways to enhance the surroundings. Public schoolteachers understand the value of bulletin boards for both information and for establishing a mood. Take time to evaluate your classroom from a student's perspective. Ask yourself if this is a place you would want to come if you weren't the teacher.

ESTABLISH THE STRATEGY

Techniques for making the classroom an enjoyable place are limitless for those who are willing to explore the options. Here are a few principles that will help you establish a strategy for fun.

1. Be willing to take a break from reality.

This principle is especially true for those who teach children. Make-believe is a world that children can relate to. Making them part of the story line will help them to internalize the message. Teens like skits and human videos that provide personal involvement without personal exposure. Adults enjoy case studies that allow them to explore the "what if" issues.

2. Use a variety of methods.

It is important to remember that not everyone learns in the same way you do. Be aware of the various learning styles in your class and devise ways to include everyone in at least some portion of the learning experience. This variation will break up any monotony that may develop and will provide the students in the room with motivation to come back again because they know they will receive something when they do.

3. Encourage movement.

Some adults will resist the idea of moving around in class, but most teens or younger students will welcome the opportunity to expend energy. Those who require their students to sit quietly in hard metal chairs virtually guarantee discipline problems and dissatisfaction on the part of both the students and the teacher. God did not create children and teens to sit for long periods of time. We must be willing to work with the characteristics God has placed within His creation, not against them.

4. Provide an example.

Students will take their cue from you. If you enjoy being in class, so will they. Smile, be friendly, have fun, and show interest in your students. Show the students that it is not only acceptable to have fun in God's house, it is required.

5. Provide tangible incentives.

Everyone enjoys prizes and rewards. Run an occasional attendance contest or offer small gifts and incentives for certain levels of involvement or guest invitation. Incentives should be obtainable by all. Do not turn rewards into subtle punishments. It is more fun when large numbers can share in the joy derived from participation by the group.

ENGAGE THE STUDENT

The teacher should not have to produce all the fun that takes place in the classroom. Students can take an active role in maintaining an atmosphere of fun in the classroom. Here are a few ways to help them do so.

1. Teach students to respect one another.

Students should have fun, but should never be allowed to embarrass or humiliate their peers. It is easy for fun to "get out of hand" and become hurtful if the teacher does not establish safeguards against disrespectful behavior. Enforcing simple rules of mutual respect should suffice to accomplish that task.

2. Involve students in the composition of the class.

Assign different aspects of the class to students who have appropriate skills for such. Let a creative teen put together a skit for the class. Have an adult who is good with crafts teach other adults how to do a craft that reinforces the lesson topic. Allow younger students to help illustrate a lesson with stories from their lives. Involving the students will make the class more enjoyable for all.

3. Offer outside activities.

Plan a minimum of four class parties each year. The goal of these parties should be pure enjoyment. Parties for the smaller children should include parents. Those in the older groups should include activities that are designed to appeal to them.

Regardless of age or maturity, people want to have a good time. Although not everything that is worthwhile in life is "fun," most people decide to participate in activities because they perceive that the time will be enjoyable. People will keep coming to a place that provides good company with others who know how to have good fun and learn something while they are at it.

IT'S HAPPENING

Glad Tidings Assembly of God located in Reading, Pennsylvania, is a place known for its fun. Debora Bube, director of Christian education, graciously shared some of the priorities and practices that make this church and its Christian education program a place that people enjoy attending.

The driving philosophy behind Glad Tiding's success is the belief that providing an atmosphere conducive to experiencing fun is important because people want to be a part of something that is worthy of their time. The goal of the leadership of Glad Tidings has been to provide a variety of activities for the children who attend Sunday School there. They have accomplished this goal through the use of Bible learning centers that provide for various learning styles and methods which incorporate the senses (arts, cooking, science, drama, games). Providing variety for adults is also a goal of the church. Adults are given options through the use of elective classes. The population of Glad Tidings adult Sunday School has doubled since they introduced elective classes. Some of the electives offered include parenting classes, Grief Share, children of divorce, foundations for new believers, Divorce Care, Marriage Builders, and stewardship classes. Glad Tidings has made it a priority to look for creative ways to present God's unchanging Word to an ever-changing world in an enjoyable manner.

When asked for specific ways Glad Tidings has encouraged an atmosphere of enjoyment, Pastor Bryan Koch shared this response: "Something that colors the teaching ministry in our church from the pulpit to the classroom is the recognition that the Bible reveals real people in real situations. The Bible is more enjoyable and fulfilling when we 'put flesh and bone' on the characters found there." He goes on to say, "this can be and is done in a variety of ways—creative illustrations, the use of humor, carefully selected personal illustrations, as well as the use of props that drive home the message or lesson. This is very similar to the manner in which Jesus taught." The leadership of Glad Tidings realize that people are more receptive to strong truth when it is presented sincerely, yet in a way that the average person can relate to. It has been the experience of the teachers and pastors of this church that those who receive God's challenges to their lives with laughter often will later find themselves weeping in repentance at the altar.

Vacation Bible School is one of the most fun and exciting times of the year for those who attend Glad Tidings. People of all ages participate in their VBS program. The adults who are helpers and teachers have as much fun as the children. The coordinators of the VBS program make sure that each VBS has a fun and exciting theme. A highlight of VBS is the willingness of all participants to dress in costume in an effort to enhance the atmosphere.

When asked to identify the single most effective element that reflects the church's emphasis on enjoyment, Bube pointed to the Pastor's Welcome Class. She states, "One of the most impacting classes that we offer is the Pastor's Welcome Class where people new to the church have enjoyed getting to know our senior pastor. Through this class, people have caught a vision for our church, learned our doctrine, discovered their spiritual gifts, and are now enjoying serving Christ in their God-given ministry." As we can see from this statement, at Glad Tidings, enjoyment is more than fun and games. Enjoyment is a product of finding fulfillment in Christ in an atmosphere that is warm, welcoming, and has the welfare of each person in mind.

Pastor Koch had this observation for churches and Sunday Schools that want to become a place people enjoy attending. "Many Christians only see Christ as 'a Man of sorrows and acquainted with grief' (Isaiah 53:5), but the Word of God reveals Christ as having been 'anointed with the oil of gladness more than your companions.'" Koch also reminds us, "Learning and teaching should not be mutually exclusive to fun and enjoyment." It is important for every Sunday School teacher and pastor to embrace this concept.

A FINAL LOOK

Dena sat in the pew alone on a Sunday night. As she looked around the sanctuary, she noted that she wasn't the only one who had a pew to herself. Just this morning the five hundred seat auditorium was nearly filled. Tonight fewer than 10 percent of that number were in attendance. She was new to the church and wondered why there was such a difference.

That evening Dena decided to find out why so few of her fellow church mates bothered to show up to worship on Sunday evening. She made a list of the people whom she wanted to talk to. During the altar time, she prayed for wisdom, strength, and courage to complete her self-assigned task.

The first person she approached was a coworker who attended the church. Dena asked Diane what she had done the night before. Diane said that she had gotten together with a few church friends and had played Rook until after ten o'clock. She said that her partner and she had won two out of three of the games they had played.

Diane returned what she perceived as pleasantries by asking Dena what she had done. Dena proudly said she had attended church. Diane smiled and said, "That must have been fun."

Dena encouraged Diane to join her at church the following Sunday evening. Diane hesitated for a moment and then told her that she really couldn't make it. She explained that Sunday nights were the best time for her and her friends to spend time together and to do some things they enjoyed.

That night Dena continued her quest by calling her friend Stan. Stan and Dena hadn't known each very long, but they had determined that they enjoyed a lot of things in common. Dena dialed his number and was greeted by a cheerful voice on the other end of the line. Dena discovered that Stan had spent Sunday evening reading the latest end-times novel by a famous Christian author. He told her of the adventures that were contained in the pages of the book. He asked her if she thought what he had read was accurate. Dena gave him her opinion and listened as he shared his excitement about the future.

Finally Stan's enthusiasm ebbed, and he asked Dena what she had done on Sunday night. When Dena told him she had been at church, he asked her what had gone on. She told him about the service. He responded, "Hope you had fun."

Dena asked Stan what he thought he would be doing the following Sunday evening. Stan quickly said that he was going to try to finish the book he had been reading. He told her that if he did finish it, there were a lot more things he would like to learn about God and that he had a long list of books that he wanted to get through. Dena could almost see Stan's eyes sparkle as he talked about his plans.

Finally, Dena asked her good friend Marsha what she did Sunday evenings that kept her away from church. Marsha smiled widely and told Dena about her weekly trips to the local nursing home. She had gone to visit a sick friend's mom one week when her friend could not make it. Marsha ended up not only spending time with her friend's mom, but with nearly every patient on that wing. Marsha walked away from that night exhilarated. She was sure that she had encouraged the patients, but she was convinced that the evening had actually benefited her more than it had them. She told Dena that there was little more that she looked forward to each week than the time she got to spend going from room to room, ministering to these precious people. "I'm having a blast," she gushed.

Dena didn't even bother to ask Marsha if she was available to go to church with her next Sunday evening. She simply smiled and walked away.

Dena was confused. She had expected that her friends didn't go to church on Sunday evenings because they were too busy. But, this didn't seem to be the case. People had enough time to go to someone's house and play games, to sit at home and read a book, or even to spend the evening at a nursing home. She had also suspected that people weren't going to the evening service because they were not sensitive to God and spiritual things. This didn't seem to be the case either. Diane obviously wanted fellowship with other believers or she wouldn't spend time with them. Stan wanted to know more about spiritual things or he wouldn't be reading the type of books that he did. And Marsha cared about ministry or she wouldn't be ministering to people in a nursing home each week. She didn't feel that she had yet determined why people weren't going to church on Sunday nights.

The following Sunday Dena read the bulletin during the opening chorus. She noted that there would be a potluck dinner the following Sunday evening at the church. She shook her head thinking about how little food there would be considering the attendance of a typical Sunday evening service. She continued reading and didn't give it another thought.

On the night of the potluck dinner, Dena brought a potato salad and fried chicken from her favorite grocer's deli for the potluck dinner. She was stunned when she looked at the parking lot of the church. It was half full. This was a far cry from the ten cars that usually resided on the ample blacktop. More cars arrived as she got out of her car. She was especially surprised when she saw Tom drive up.

The fellowship hall of the church was filled with happy voices and smiling faces. Right in the middle of a large group was her friend Diane. She waved to Dena and invited her to join the group.

After the pastor prayed, everyone got in line to wait to sample the entrees. There was a short song service, the pastor gave a talk, and people lingered well beyond the ending time of a normal Sunday evening service.

As Dena walked away that evening, she thought about the research she had done and the events of the evening. Finally, it all made sense. People want to have fun.

4

They want to meet God.

"One hundred religious persons knit into unity by careful organization do not constitute a church any more than eleven dead men make a football team. The first requisite is life, always."

A. W. Tozer

His day had begun like most mornings did.

The servants were lighting lamps, slowly dispelling the dark haze that had settled in the temple. Sunshine from the outer court seldom penetrated the shadows within the inner court until at least noon. The lamps would help, but the room was always shrouded in a gray fog throughout the morning.

It somehow seemed symbolic to the old priest. There hadn't been much brightness in Israel either. God, it seemed, had forgotten them. The promises of the ancient prophets had become folktales to most Jews. The priesthood was ruled more by corruption than by any real hope of Messiah. Lighting the lamps had become meaningless and the ceremonies little more than an exercise in futility.

Why had the God who had led their people in days past chosen to abandon them? It had been centuries since the last visitation. The old priest knew there was no answer, and he chided himself for allowing his mind to wander there again. It was pointless. Even the debates about God had become familiar and unfulfilling. Daily bread was about the only reason to maintain the charade in the temple.

The shuffling of feet behind him stirred the priest from his thoughts. He turned to find it was only Anna. He smirked and shook his head as she pattered by him, mumbling her endless prayers. The old woman lifted a bony hand above her head, offering a stream of praise toward the heavens. The sight was as routine as the daily lighting of the lamps.

Why bother? The words almost escaped his lips. He sighed with relief that his own frustration hadn't spilled onto the prophetess Anna. There was no sense in spreading his depression to one so determined to believe. Still it seemed a sad picture as he watched the shriveled woman shuffle back and forth, begging God for a day that they'd never see.

Of course, not everyone lived under the gray skies of his doubt. There were several fools who continued to believe the day of the Messiah and His kingdom was near. Each generation had its own crazy zealots who would see to that. *People will believe anything if it means an end to this Roman nightmare,* he thought. He shook his head at the foolishness. Such ideas would end in bitter disappointment soon enough.

And then there was Simeon. The old man had stirred up a few people himself. He wasn't a rabble-rouser like some of the others, but his insistence that God would allow him to live until the day of the Messiah excited more than a few—especially now that he had grown old.

The priest slowly scanned the room before him. Sadness engulfed him as it had done so often. It wasn't that he wanted to give up. He really wanted to believe. For years he'd been among those watching and hoping for the consolation of Israel. But the years had turned to decades, and the faint hope in his heart had grown as feeble as his body. "Where are You, God," he wanted to scream, but only Anna's songs of praise filled the room.

A shadow appeared in the doorway. The silhouette of Simeon was framed by the sunlight. Anna looked up in surprise. "What is it?" the priest called, bracing himself for another meaningless debate.

"I'm not certain," came the puzzled reply. "The Spirit of God has brought me here."

The priest looked hard at Simeon. While he had never accepted Simeon's hope of seeing the Messiah, he knew the old man was generally sensible and he highly honored the temple leaders.

"Come," the priest beckoned. "Tell me what the Spirit of God has said to you."

Simeon stepped into the room and followed the priest to a table and chairs. But before another word was spoken, the silhouette of a couple appeared in the doorway.

"He has come," Simeon whispered, his eyes blazing with excitement. The volume of Anna's praises across the room seemed to increase.

"Who...who has come?" the old priest's voice was uncertain.

Simeon had already moved toward the door and now stood with the man and his wife. She cradled an infant in her arms.

The priest longed to join them, but his feet seemed riveted to the floor. Simeon now cradled the child against his bony chest. Suddenly his voice filled the room. "Sovereign Lord, as you have promised, you now dismiss your servant in peace. For my eyes have seen your salvation."

The old priest crumbled to the floor, a mixture of awe and unbelief. *Could this be? Could this really be?* he wondered. Everything within him wanted to believe, but no words would come. His shoulders shook with emotion, and tears rushed to the ground just inches from his face. Simeon's voice continued his proclamation above the old priest's sobs.

Soon Anna's voice joined the celebration, proclaiming remarkable prophecies over the infant child. Scrambling to his feet, the priest drew closer to the scene, being observed by the overwhelmed faces of the couple.

"Do you mean?" the priest finally managed.

A smile danced across Simeon's face. A song of praise burst from his lips, bringing a beautiful harmony to the melody of Anna's stream of praise. The old priest stared at the quiet face of the child. *Could this really be Him?* His thoughts spun faster than he could form words. "Is it...You?"

The child seemed oblivious to his question, but the hope suddenly alive in the old priest mounted undeterred. Was this the day he would finally meet God?

The warmth of the noonday sun washed across him, bringing a glow to the entire room.

*A*ccording to research, 95 percent of Americans believe in God. Only 68 percent identify Him as the all-powerful, all-knowing, perfect Creator of the universe who rules the world today, indicating that nearly one-third of our population has ideas of God that differ from those of traditional Christianity. But they believe in God, a Creator, One who is above all others.[1]

The same research reveals that 85 percent of Americans consider themselves Christians.[2] Few of us are ready to proclaim that such numbers indicate we're reaching the end of our evangelism assignment, but they do provide a fascinating window into the American mind. God is out there, and, on some level, we identify with Him.

It has long been the contention of Christian theology that men and women were created to know God. Indeed, the origins described in the Bible's initial book reveal clearly that mankind was formed in the image of God in order to enjoy fellowship and relationship with the Creator. Of course, it took less than three chapters for that relationship to be damaged, and the remaining 1,186 chapters of the Bible describe God's plan and action to restore it.

But while God's desire for relationship is richly evident in those chapters, one must ask if mankind shares the same desire. Most of us would quickly answer "yes," confident that no man, woman, or child is complete until the vacancy in his or her heart is filled by the One it was made for. Unfortunately, most of these incomplete lives seem oblivious to their much-needed solution. Still, they believe in Him, at a rate of 95 percent.

Aside from those who have yet to identify their desire for that relationship with God, thousands of others drift into sanctuaries or tune to religious programming for that very reason. The possibility of meeting God is what sets the Church apart from other activities, clubs, or events in your community. Church has long been referred to as God's house, and many who enter are hoping to find Him at home.

It is absolutely legitimate for your students to enter your classroom with the expectation of meeting God. That's why you're there. And that expectation forms the distinctive purpose of the ministry of your church. Every other chapter in this book describes a need that can be met in other settings as well. But the desire to meet God leads an individual to church. And a desire to know Him more fully motivates the trek to your classroom.

They need to meet God. Their presence in your classroom likely indicates that they want to meet God. Yours is the privilege to facilitate that opportunity.

MAKING IT HAPPEN

Where did you meet God? While some Christians may have a unique story of apparent coincidences that led them to discovering God's love, most of us found God because of the intentional effort of someone else. Of course, we understand that by "finding God," we do not imply that we initiated the search. God lovingly reached out to each of us and initiated the very possibility of a relationship through Christ's sacrifice.

But at some point, we discovered the availability of that relation-ship with God and responded to the opportunity. In most cases, it is because of the intentional act of a friend, family member, or ministry leader that people meet God. It is that opportunity and how we help create it for others that takes focus in this chapter.

EMBRACE THE NEED

Can students meet God in your class? Before offering a simple "yes," give thought to the magnitude of your answer. Is it conceivable that the Creator of the universe will come to meet with a student amid the plaster and paint of your classroom? The answer IS "yes," but what an incredible thought. And, there are a few other thoughts you must con-sider if your students are to meet God in your Sunday School.

1. What are you preparing for?

The difference between preparing for class and preparing to meet God may seem to be little more than semantics to some. But such limited expectations may cause you to miss the whole point of the ministry God has given you. A prepared teacher most certainly includes study and mastery of methods to make the lesson most effective. But there's more to preparation. Much more!

Teachers who guide their students toward meeting God start by meeting with God themselves. Sunday is about more than dispensing a lesson. It is about life change—a moment with God that results in a life forever altered. Teachers must be prepared by seeking God and His direction and heart for each student. Results come from opportu-nities, and opportunities never occur apart from expectation. What are you anticipating God to do through His Word and your teaching?

2. What is the role of prayer?

There are no more powerful moments of preparation for the

teacher than those spent in prayer. We are God's servants, seeking to see His agenda fulfilled in the lives of our students. That's a teacher's reason for being.

Such moments with God result from prayer. While our teaching ability may inspire or enlighten, the great moments of meeting with God come on a different level. Consider keeping the names of your students on a notepad so you can pray throughout the week for God to meet each individual.

3. Do your students see Christ in you?

As a teacher, you are an ambassador or representative of our Savior. It is no accident that many small children form their earliest impressions of God by the lives of their pastors or Sunday School teachers. Your students need to meet God when they come to your class. They also need to meet His disciple—you. Commit yourself daily to living the life you teach them. If your students see God's love in you, they will be better prepared to meet with God.

ENHANCE THE ENVIRONMENT

Can you create an environment where your students will meet God? Some teachers may believe they have a limited role in this area, and certainly we know that God doesn't need a classroom to draw your students to Him. But there are some environmental issues to consider.

1. Do your students expect the supernatural?

To those who have yet to experience God's presence, God is often believed to be a distant being with a limited interest in individuals. Since we know this is not accurate, we must help our students understand God's desire to meet with them.

76

Again, the key is expectation. We do not seek to manufacture a mystical environment or any confusing idea of a cosmic encounter. Rather, we know God is a loving Father who delights in relationship with each of us. That is the God we study and the God we want to meet with and learn of every week.

We often speak of church as God's house. While we certainly understand that such ideas are not intended to limit where God can be found, your students need to expect to find Him "at home." When they come to your class anticipating both a lesson and an encounter with God, they are then open and ready for the work God wants to do in their lives.

2. Who's doing the talking?

It's a simple thought, really. A class where people can meet God is a place where teachers and students aren't the only ones talking. Teach your students to listen to God through His Word and through prayer. Give opportunities during class for these elements of relationship with God.

ESTABLISH THE STRATEGY

While the key element of environment is expectation, there are strategies you can implement that reveal your expectation of God's meeting you and your students in class. Consider these.

1. Give opportunities.

For years Sunday School was one of the local church's most effective evangelistic ministries. More people received Christ in Sunday School than in any other ministry effort. However, in many places today the Sunday School has lost its effectiveness in evangelism. The reason? Often opportunity is lacking.

The small group study of God's Word yields many exciting moments of understanding God and His plan for our lives. But we must move beyond understanding to experience. If you are describing God's love in salvation, opportunity should be given to receive. If you are teaching about God's power to heal, what better moment than to seek God's healing for those in need.

Discipleship is never a mere intellectual pursuit. God has revealed himself through His Word so that we can experience Him, not just so that we can study the experiences of others. As a teacher, you reveal your expectations by the opportunities you give.

2. Include elements of worship.

Worship is fundamentally a response to God. Your students will respond to opportunities to worship God. Pause after conveying a key principle and invite your students to speak a sentence of thanksgiving to God. Let them write a few sentences to communicate their thoughts about what they are learning. If facilities and abilities allow, lead your class in a familiar chorus that provides a response to what you are learning. Any response you help your students make to God will teach them to worship and praise Him.

3. Share your journey.

There's nothing like an experienced traveler to be a guide on a journey. You've experienced God and His love, so share those moments with your students. Your experiences will help them see that an invitation into God's presence is theirs as well. And if you take time every day to meet with God, soon they'll have the same desire as you share about your journey.

4. Understand the role of Scripture.

The Bible is much more than an ancient book with all the answers.

It is God's written revelation of himself to us. When we encounter the Bible, we see God speaking to us through its pages and through the applications the Holy Spirit helps us make to our lives.

Too many Christians see the Bible as a book they are supposed to read. As a teacher, you can present a much different perspective. The Bible is a living guide for our relationship with God and a key way God speaks to our lives. Help your students see that they can meet with God through His Word.

5. Don't miss meetings with God.

When altar times occur during worship services or other events, watch for the response of your students. If they respond to God, be among those who encourage and pray with them in those moments. As a teacher, you are a participant in spiritual leadership in your students' lives. Don't limit your participation to the classroom. Be involved in every moment of spiritual growth that you can.

ENGAGE THE STUDENT

No one wants God to meet with your students more than God does! Think of that! Meeting with your students is His agenda. For us, the key elements include expectation and opportunity. We don't make such moments happen, but we can help open the way for God to work in our students' lives.

1. The classroom altar.

You may not have space for a physical altar in your classroom, but be certain that your room is more than a place of study. It is a place to meet God. Always provide opportunity for students to meet with God in your class. We study His Word to know Him, not merely to know about Him. Make every class period an opportunity to grow closer to God.

2. The habit of response.

When your students learn to respond to God in class, they will respond to Him and His direction in many situations. Christianity is not a spectator sport. All students must respond to God, and they will if we include opportunities for response in our teaching.

3. The highlight of your hour.

What is the greatest moment in the classroom? Is it the game everyone enjoyed or the incredible creativity of your methodology? Such moments are wonderful, but they are easily surpassed by those moments when God meets with your students. Seeing a student experience God's love, forgiveness, and new life is what makes teaching a remarkable joy.

People want to meet God. They have many different ideas of who He is or what such a meeting would be like. But you've been there. God has changed your life. Expect Him to change the lives of your students too. It will be the highlight of your class.

IT'S HAPPENING

First Assembly of God located in North Little Rock, Arkansas, places a high priority on providing opportunities for people to meet God in their services and their Sunday School classrooms. Following are insights gained from an interview with pastoral staff member John Long.

The major emphasis at First Assembly of North Little Rock is that people do not leave the same as when they arrived at church. They believe this is made possible when people are in the presence of God, not just as a corporate group of believers, but also as individuals. Thus the leaders of this church strive to provide an environment where visitors and members are in His presence. Sunday

School is an important agency in this process as members learn practical application of biblical truths and experience the love of Christ and the presence of the Holy Spirit.

All of the Sunday School related programs at First Assembly are designed to meet the practical needs of people, regardless of their age or phase of life. Examples of this include classes offered for those in college, those going through divorce, those dealing with grief, and those who are caring for terminally ill family members. The leadership emphasizes that people who are growing in their relationship with God, connecting to the body of believers, serving God and others, and sharing their beliefs and experiences with others will be helped to maintain a proper perspective regardless of what is transpiring in their lives.

John Long shared the following story that provides one example of how a visitor to the church encountered God in a Sunday School class. "A lady came to 'First Look' (a church and Sunday School orientation class offered by the church). She had just left her husband and was very upset about that. She had a two-year-old and wanted the family to be reunited, but she felt it was best for her son if she remained separated. She was unfamiliar with the things of God. She asked if you could pray for a specific thing, such as asking God to help her husband. That morning a couple who had experienced marital problems was leading the class. I shared with her that the wife started attending First Assembly alone, and she had asked that we pray for her unsaved husband. I then pointed to her husband and said, 'See that guy standing over there? That's her husband; he's hosting the class today.' She began to cry, very deep sobs. When she gained her composure, she looked up to me and said, 'So, this really works?' This was a true God moment."

When asked for hints that could help other churches and Sunday Schools foster an expectancy of meeting God in their classes, Long provided the following suggestions: Although everyone is different, there are similarities. "First, take the time and effort to get to know the needs and desires of the people. This is best done by talking with the Sunday School leadership as well as 'key' members of each class. Although God never changes, the world does, and there needs to be a constant effort to find different mediums to introduce the lost to Christ and to encourage the saved to grow in Him."

Brother Long concludes by stating, "Emphasis must always be on the person's relationship with God through Bible study, prayer and fasting, and service to others." When this approach is taken, people will focus on an encounter with a living God rather than simply coming to church and Sunday School for a theology lesson.

A FINAL LOOK

Becky sat in her room silently staring into space. The events of the past few hours raced through her mind. She was confused and hurt, but strangely she felt that something happened that night that would change her life forever.

Becky had just returned from what her friend called a "revival service" at her friend's church. There was lots of good music followed by an energetic message about experiencing God. The topic was exciting to Becky because she had always wanted to know what it was like to have an encounter with God. At the end of his message, the preacher challenged people to come to the front of the room and seek God. Becky eagerly joined the crowd as it moved forward.

A man stood in front of Becky crying uncontrollably. To her side was an older woman shouting words that Becky couldn't quite understand. A thumping sound came from somewhere across the auditorium. Becky looked in that direction to see about ten people jumping up and down. People all around her were shouting and singing. Becky stood among those people and experienced nothing. As the spiritual fervor began to diminish, Becky wandered back to her seat in much the same condition she was in when she left it.

After church, Becky joined her friend and others who attended the church service for a late-night snack. The conversation quickly turned to what they called "a tremendous move of God." Her friend Jen said that she felt God had spoken to her that night and had given her guidance concerning a decision she needed to make. Larry talked about the joy he felt after spending time in prayer. Dave seemed to be glowing as he talked about His exciting encounter with God. Becky sat silent, eating her hamburger and fries.

When Becky's roommate got home, she saw Becky's light on and decided to go into her room to say good night. Amy knocked, but got no response. She opened the door and was momentarily frightened when she saw the near comatose look on Becky's face. Amy cautiously moved over to where Becky sat and touched her shoulder. Becky's startled body jerked as she acknowledged Amy's touch. When Amy asked her if there was anything she could do, Becky just shook her head. She said nothing.

After Amy left the room, Becky began to cry softly. She wondered what was wrong with her. Why did this God that Jen claimed to serve reveal himself to everyone else, while He seemed to ignore her? Did she do something wrong when she went up front tonight? Didn't the pastor say that all she had to do was listen and God would speak to her, to ask and she would receive? Had she failed to listen intently enough? Had she asked incorrectly? Did God not love her? She fell asleep that night wondering what she had to do to make God reveal himself to her.

The next morning the previous evening's events were still gripping Becky's thoughts. Amy came to the table and asked if Becky was ready to talk about the issues that consumed her the night before. Becky nodded. She began to relate her story. Amy could not fully relate to Becky's concerns, but she listened patiently.

Neither Becky nor Amy attended church regularly. Last night Becky had gone to the revival service as a favor to her friend. Becky's life hadn't been going great, and she had always thought it would be neat to have an encounter with God. When Jen had mentioned that supernatural things were happening at her church, she eagerly chose to go. In some ways she wished that she had never said yes.

Seeing how upset Becky was, Amy suggested that the two of them explore ways to make contact with this mystical being that people called God. Amy assured Becky that she too would like to meet God, but she said she didn't really want to have to go to church or become a Christian to do so. Becky was a little skeptical about looking for God anyplace after her recent experience, but she agreed to journey a little further in her quest for God.

The two women began their search by surfing the Internet. They were surprised at the vast amount of material they found related to God and spirituality. They scanned through material that explained God in terms of pantheism, Islam, Mormonism, Judaism, and even atheism. One particular area caught their attention. This was the philosophical belief system that was followed by people who called themselves Zen Buddhists. Becky and Amy found over seven hundred articles on the subject. They downloaded many of the articles on meditation and began to put some of the principles into practice.

After a few weeks of studying Zen and practicing the mental exercises associated with it, Becky became discouraged again. She felt relaxed after her spiritual sessions, but she failed to have the encounter with God that she so desperately sought. She surrendered her hope for finding God through meditation, but not her quest for God.

The two women continued their journey toward spiritual reality by pursuing the New Age philosophy in which a few of their friends at work were involved. They bought crystals and sought unity with the universe; this too brought no lasting satisfaction. Like a rat in a maze, Amy and Becky went down one dead-end alley after another, failing to find the reward that awaited them if they could simply find the right path.

Each time Becky began to explore a new avenue to God, her mind went back to that Sunday evening so many months before. She couldn't shake the feeling that the people she had eaten with after church had found what she was seeking. She also knew that although she had not understood the things that happened around her at the front of the church, she had seen a peace in that church service that she had not found in her other spiritual quests.

ENDNOTES

[1]Barna Research Group, Ltd. (1997). *Beliefs: General Religious,* [Online]. Available FTP: www.barna.org

[2]Ibid.

5

*They want
to be
understood.*

"As we mature spiritually, we exhibit a growing capacity to care for and appreciate one another in the body of Christ, regardless of our differences."

Joseph Stowell

The sun bore down like only a desert midday sun can. Water pots clanged together at her side, leaving a small trail of chipped fragments along the road. The pottery was cheap, but if that's all one has, well . . .

Beads of perspiration coiled down the side of her face, trickling down her back until the glaring heat vaporized them into oblivion. It was hot. Every inch of the road seemed to have braced itself for its daily scorching. Little wonder no one made the journey for water at this time of day. No one, that is, except the frail body now shuffling on the path.

Tired fingers clutched the water pots loosely, saving their strength for the more strenuous return trip. Bare feet covered with dust angled among the rocks, vainly searching for the coolness of a patch of grass. Had one pulled back the cloak that covered her face like a shroud, the sadness of her eyes would be overwhelming. Little wonder. Only a woman such as this would go to the well at midday.

Two men, with hands free, passed by swiftly on her right. They offered no help, but rather shot brief looks of scorn in her direction. One spit in the path right in front of her, and soon they were gone. Their hatred brought no response from her. Such things had become all too familiar. The life she lived had brought condemnation from many more than these two.

No one really understood. Was it her fault that her drunken, controlling, and abusive father had spiraled her in a never-ending search for love? Was she to blame for trusting the wrong men—

89

men who promised her the care she needed only to prove themselves to be just like her father? How could she become a proper woman when no righteous man would ever choose to care for her?

It was her fault. Instinctively she knew it. All the gossip. All the stares. She had decided she deserved it all. Still, a small hope flickered that someday, somewhere, someone would love her the way she deserved to be loved.

It certainly wasn't the man she had left in bed this morning. The bruise below her left eye said that clearly enough. Of course, the fact that he still refused to marry her should have told her sooner. But she needed a roof over her head even if she couldn't have a marriage certificate. Still, that hope flickered. She was still young, though lines of regret and pain had already marked her face.

The well was just a few steps away when she saw Him. He was sitting behind the well at an angle almost hidden by the massive stones. His presence startled her. She was not used to company at the well . . . and she didn't want any. Her heart longed to run, but her legs refused. She would have to endure His scorn or face her man's rage if she returned empty-handed.

She hurriedly poured water into the first pot, hoping He would simply ignore her. And for a moment, she thought He would. But then a voice, not harsh and accusing, but kind and a bit weary spoke to her.

"Will you give me a drink?"

His request caught her off guard. *You've got to be kidding,* she wanted to scream. Did this Jew know nothing of the way things were? Nothing of the hatred between their peoples? Nothing of . . . her?

"You are a Jew and I am a Samaritan woman," she protested.

His eyes showed no offense at her rebuke. He actually seemed to smile. "If you knew the gift of God and who it is that asks you for a drink, you would have asked him and he would have given you living water."

The water pot clanged to the ground, spilling its precious contents across both their feet. "Sir, you have nothing to draw with," she heard herself say. Her words were no longer sharp as His kindness seemed to envelop her.

"Everyone who drinks this water will be thirsty again, but whoever drinks the water I give him will never thirst. Indeed, the water I give him will become in him a spring of water welling up to eternal life." His eyes flashed with truth, while the emotion inside her surged like a volcano, reaching the surface only in the tears that formed around her eyes.

"Sir, give me this water so that I won't get thirsty and have to keep coming here to draw water." A hot surge of wind blew across her feet, drying the last of the water she had spilled. *Who was this?* she wondered. There was something in His eyes, in His smile, that she'd never seen before. Surely if He knew her, He wouldn't speak so kindly.

"Go, call your husband and come back," the man spoke again.

Tears poured freely now. "I have no husband," she sobbed. Lowering her eyes, she waited for His rebuke.

But no rebuke came. "You are right," He said softly. "You have had five husbands and the man you now have is not your husband." He knew. He knew about . . . He knew everything!

How . . . She wanted to know how He knew, but the question caught in her throat. It could have been the gossips, but this man was a stranger. Who would have thought her wicked story important enough to tell to this Jew? There had to be another reason.

At that moment, the flicker of hope within found strength. Could this be? Could He be? Her head spun with thoughts she had never expected. He knew her. Somehow He knew her. And yet there was no hatred in His eyes.

"I can see that you are a prophet," she managed. His smile derailed her. She fought the urge to trust Him. "We worship on

91

this mountain, but you Jews claim we must worship in Jerusalem." The age-old conflict was her only defense against eyes that seemed to see right through her.

Again He was kind, not rebuking. The words of His answer flowed past her, though her real question was much deeper.

"I know that Messiah is coming," she almost whispered. "When he comes, he will explain everything to us," she finished, expecting the conversation to end. She turned back to the water pot at her feet and lifted the drawing basin to the mouth of the well.

"I who speak to you am he."

She stopped. This time the larger vessel tumbled to the ground, just ahead of the tears that now flowed freely. She was right! It was the Christ!

She turned and looked into the tender eyes of Messiah! He knew everything! He understood everything! Her shoulders shook with sobs as years of pain evaporated in the desert heat. She turned to speak, but a group of men were approaching. Suddenly she felt a freedom and love welling up within her.

Water pots scattered as she scampered away, back toward the village. A fire of hope and peace now roared inside her, and it was too great to contain.

Mouths of neighbors gaped as she approached. Women who would cross the road to avoid her had no time to escape. Frowns of disdain exploded into anger, but it didn't matter to her anymore. "Come!" she shouted. "Come see a man who told me everything I ever did!"

"Come meet the Messiah!" She shouted, laughing with joy.

*O*ne of the most frequent descriptions the Gospel writers make about the physical person of Jesus relates to His eyes. There are no poetic descriptions such as "pools of eternal love" or any detailed information about eye color, but His eyes held a fascination for His contemporaries. They were simply described as eyes of compassion.

There were many reasons to join the band of disciples who followed the Son of God across the Judean hillsides. His eyes of compassion certainly make the list. Many abandoned successful careers, years of habits, even family inheritances to follow Him. Of course, some followed hoping He would rebel against Rome, and others joined the group grateful for healing or deliverance. But many followed Him because of what they saw in His eyes—compassion, the product of understanding.

You see, eyes of compassion communicate understanding. Jesus knew. He knew their hurts. He knew their longings. He knew they felt alone and lost. He knew they were oppressed. On many occasions, He revealed that He even knew their thoughts. He could have used this incredible knowledge to control or manipulate people for selfish goals, but He used it only to love. Each of them, from the woman caught in adultery to the tax collector who was miserable amid his millions, needed understanding, and they found it in this unique Galilean.

It should interest us greatly that in the most intense discussion Christ held with His disciples, He offered the strong focus to "Love one another." In fact, this three-word command took center stage in His final hours with them. It is clear that Jesus believed this command was the glue that would hold His Commission and their survival together.

Life has changed greatly since people traveled a few miles in dusty sandals. Today we can cross the globe at a speed that would make Simon Peter dizzy. Through technology we can link to millions without leaving our kitchen table. We walk . . . only for exercise.

But our need for understanding is as intense as ever. The eyes of compassion still hold their appeal.

Knowledge has exploded. We now have access to more knowledge than we could use in a lifetime. The information highway offers more destinations than the mind can comprehend. Yet amid all this knowledge, people long to be understood. We can diagnose them, predict their responses to circumstances, even offer clinical explanations for their feelings, but the understanding that soothes the heart on its deepest levels remains aloof.

Some come looking for that understanding in the same places the ancient disciples looked. They enter church buildings curious to understand God, but perhaps more desperate to discover if He knows them. What do you suppose they find?

If they find "one-size-fits-all" approaches to their needs, they will soon take their quest elsewhere. But if they find love and concern for their individual circumstances, they may stay a lifetime.

They want understanding. People today are still looking for eyes of compassion. Will they find them in church?

MAKING IT HAPPEN

Ours is a culture of high expectations. We expect satisfactory food service in a fraction of a minute. We expect the article of clothing that makes us look good to be immediately available in our size. And, we expect a ride to work if we are going to honor a mechanic with the opportunity to fix our car. Simply put, we have grown accustomed to being taken care of with excellence or taking our needs to someone else.

Welcome to human nature. Each of us, regardless of our depth of maturity or sanctification, wrestles against the urge to view each moment of life through the lens of "how it affects me." And in a day when commitment is given only in exchange for value, this self-centered aspect of human nature is ever more visible. For many people who enter our churches and classrooms, nearly every experience is weighed on the scale of personal benefit. What's in it for me? How will I benefit? What will I gain from attending church and Sunday School? These attitudes are the essence of our human nature.

Think of it this way. People come to Sunday School, not merely to learn the content of God's Word; they expect to discover its relevance for their lives right now. Thankfully, the Bible can deliver on such demands, but every teacher must understand the expectations of the student. Factual understanding is not enough for today's students. Relevance for their lives is demanded. And the student expects his own needs and circumstances to be understood—even addressed.

EMBRACE THE NEED

It's a big challenge, isn't it? Each week a sea of faces sits before you, each with her own story, his own set of interests, and a myriad of circumstances in need of God's understanding and help. These students need to be known, to be understood, to be helped in a uniquely personal way, and they are desperate for you to deliver.

How? Let's start again with the heart of the teacher because success begins with your own priorities.

1. Do you know your students?

Where do they come from? What do they enjoy? What do their worlds look like outside of your church building? What adversities or concerns do they encounter? While it is always God who meets our students' needs, we can be effective in teaching toward our students and their needs as we get better acquainted.

Making the effort to get to know your students creates a bond between you and them that will facilitate your teaching. You become more than just a person who students see for an hour of lecture each week. Such personal knowledge creates a relationship of trust and loyalty that enhances your efforts to disciple them. Understanding their needs will help you apply God's Word to their lives.

2. Do you believe in your students?

The need to be understood often brings an even greater desire— the hunger to be believed in. What could God do with each life in your class? What potential do you see?

Ask a group of adults about a favorite high school teacher, and they'll identify one almost immediately. Ask them what made that teacher their favorite, and the majority will describe this very point. He/She took interest in me and believed in me. In most cases, those students worked harder for that teacher than any other. We want people, especially our leaders, to believe in us.

It's remarkable how students will meet our expectations. If you expect a student to be disruptive or even obnoxious, he'll probably meet your expectation. But if you believe the best about him, he may well spend his energy trying to prove you right.

ENHANCE THE ENVIRONMENT

Once you've armed yourself with a knowledge of and a belief in your students, you're ready to tackle some environmental issues.

1. Does everyone feel included?

If a student doesn't feel like a part of your group, he doesn't feel understood. Make an effort to include each student in the class family.

Inclusion is communicated through every act and activity of the class. Does everyone know my name? Do they care about my needs? Are they interested in my opinions and ideas? As teachers, we must be sensitive to the need for inclusion during fellowship, prayer time, class discussions, and other key moments of interaction. And, that may occasionally mean making special effort to reach out to students who don't enter in easily on their own. Strategies to achieve this will be discussed in the next section.

2. Do your students feel safe?

Is your class a safe place? Your students need one. A safe place is one where they can be themselves without fear of ridicule or reprisal. They don't have to pretend to be something they're not. In a safe place, they can express their thoughts, share their fears, and find love and acceptance in spite of their shortcomings. That's a place every student needs and will gladly spend time in.

Such an environment is built intentionally. While we want to prohibit unfair behavior when it occurs, the most effective strategy includes overt statements of acceptance.

"I want each of you to know how much I care about you."

"I want our class to be a place where you can be honest about how you feel."

"No question is a foolish question."

"I want this to be a place where you feel safe and loved."

Such statements create expectation and will, over time, establish the environment they project. Of course, you need to act on them yourself. Avoid any responses to students that would send a different message.

ESTABLISH THE STRATEGY

While an environment of understanding will take time to build, there are practical, intentional strategies that will help you gain some immediate results too.

1. Recognize and use abilities.

The ability to contribute communicates belonging to most students. Effective teachers in the children's classroom give a "job" to each student. Teachers of older students find similar success when they recognize a student's interests or abilities and incorporate them into the classroom.

2. Highlight individuals.

Seems simple enough, but individual attention communicates understanding. Consider having special prayer for a different student each week. Maybe a student-of-the-week approach can help you highlight the life, activities, or hobbies of your students. Games that allow students to learn more about each other can also contribute.

While you'll want to avoid any approaches that might make some students uncomfortable, most will enjoy or appreciate appropriate individual attention within the group. It's important to let new students see others experience such attention before placing them in the "spotlight."

3. Understand and meet emotional needs.

The most effective approach in providing understanding is probably the targeting of emotional needs. While we speak more often of needs that are physical, financial, or spiritual in nature, your students are driven by their emotional needs.

A good example can be drawn from a class of three-year-olds. Suppose Megan is a first-time student in the class, and you are her new teacher. Minutes after arriving in this new room filled with a dozen unfamiliar faces, Megan's mother waves good-bye and leaves her in foreign territory. Her probable response? Tears. Megan needs security, and her key provider of this emotional need has left the room to attend an adult class. What will you do?

You could ignore Megan's need and try to teach, but her sobbing will hinder your efforts. Naturally, your efforts will immediately focus on Megan's need. She may spend the first morning on your lap or in the arms of a loving coworker, but you'll be able to teach her and the others once she feels secure in your class.

Amazingly, six weeks later Megan will see you across the sanctuary on a Sunday night and enthusiastically sprint toward you with arms open, shouting, "Teacher! Teacher!" She will now willingly abandon her mother's hand to say hi to you because you have also met her need for security.

Students of all ages are a blend of four key emotional needs—security, identity, acceptance, and significance. In different phases of life, one of these will emerge as the most dominant, but they are all with us continually. For the small child, security is forefront. But soon elementary school students will move identity to the top of the list. The effective third grade teacher finds ways to help her students feel good about themselves as they discover what they're good at.

Adolescence prioritizes acceptance to the point that some teens will even do things they don't want to do or become people they don't want to be just to gain acceptance. How much better it is for them to find the needed acceptance in the safe place of your class.

By the time we reach adulthood, the hunger for significance has taken center stage. Adults want to know their lives matter. They want their opinions to count. They are looking for ways they can stand out from the crowd and be appreciated for their unique contribution.

When teachers are able to help meet the emotional needs of students, the need for understanding is also achieved. Know your students' needs. You may want to recruit a few helpers to do nothing but help you target such needs. Train your coworkers to prioritize these emotional needs, and your students will find what they're looking for in your class.

4. Be ready for anything.

If your students are to feel understood, they may bring you needs that are overwhelming. Be sure to know what you can handle and what you cannot. At all times, fervent prayer and a referral strategy can help. Always remember that it is God who meets the needs of our students, not us, though He will often use our dedicated efforts.

A referral strategy is a simple plan for handling those needs that your time or expertise can't address. Ask your pastor or Sunday School leader to help you with such a plan.

ENGAGE THE STUDENT

Teaching is a ministry, not a task. Christ's compassion and love for those who came to Him offers the ideal demonstration of the heart of a teacher.

Students want to be understood. Their unique, and sometimes frightening, circumstances are desperate for the love and compassion of Christ. His Church is the oasis of hope they need. The role of the Sunday School teacher is not simply a matter of dispensing one-hour lessons for mass consumption. You are the emissary of love your students need in their lives.

IT'S HAPPENING

Capitol Hill Assembly of God located in Oklahoma City, Oklahoma, provides an example of a church that has had success in creating an accepting and understanding attitude toward those in its community. Associate Pastor David White's response to questions regarding the church's success in this area provides guidance for all those who wish to follow their example.

When asked about keys to developing an accepting and understanding Christian education program, Pastor White identified the openness and involvement of the laity as primary. People in the church have a willingness to give of themselves without demanding reward or repayment.

The Oklahoma City tornado of 1999 devastated a portion of the city but provided an opportunity for the people of Capitol Hill Assembly to touch the needs of its community. The youth of the church were especially active in this ministry endeavor as they entered the storm-damaged areas. They helped anyone in need, regardless of background or belief system.

There are ministries at Capitol Hill Assembly that are designed to reach out to those who often feel unaccepted. "Helping Hands" ministry has been organized to give aid and support to senior citizens and single parents. A deaf church is located in their facilities. A support group for those with prostheses meets at the church monthly. And the church has a VBS each year that is promoted throughout the community. The leadership of Capitol Hill Assembly purposely looks for opportunities to offer ministry to all types of people in loving and practical ways.

Pastor White feels that an important component of developing a feeling of acceptance and understanding is the willingness to listen to all people. He stated, "One of the goals of giving instruction in a teaching setting is to glean feedback from all of those who are in the class. The atmosphere of acceptance and understanding is vital to discovering and ministering to the needs of people."

Pastor White concluded by saying, "Capitol Hill does not hang the traditional sign out to advertise that we accept everyone regardless of race, color, etc., but we are blessed to have a growing number of Hispanic, Black, and Oriental believers come to worship with us. We try to promote through our actions that we are willing to offer acceptance and understanding to anyone."

Capitol Hill Assembly intentionally models the approach of Jesus. The people of Capitol Hill are instructed in the importance of identifying needs around them, preparing ministry plans to meet those needs, and then expending personal time and resources to reach out and touch all people. This church could be an example to motivate other churches to evaluate their efforts in this important area of acceptance and understanding. It could represent a guide for reflecting those efforts more fully toward those God has placed in a church's circle of influence.

A FINAL LOOK

Paul sat outside the vice principal's office wondering why he had been called. He couldn't think of what he might have done this time.

As Paul waited, he thought about his previous encounters with the vice principal. Last time Mr. Smith didn't even bother to call Paul's parents. He just shook his head and said there was no hope for Paul. He warned Paul that if he continued down this road, he would end up in jail for the rest of his life. Paul tried to explain that he hadn't meant to break the sink, but Mr. Smith didn't seem to believe that a person could smash hard, cold porcelain unintentionally. Paul left the office with the warning that if he committed one more offense that year, he would be expelled from school.

Paul had always had problems in school. He wasn't a very good reader, and his concentration level was very low. Paul's aptitude tests indicated that he was a very bright boy, but his teachers never saw evidence of that fact. The inconsistency between Paul's potential and his achievement led everyone to believe that he was lazy. Most people agreed with Mr. Smith; there was little hope for Paul. Fortunately, one person in Paul's life didn't feel that way: Mr. Spencer.

Mr. Spencer was Paul's Sunday School teacher. It was strange, but in Mr. Spencer's class Paul seldom had trouble. It wasn't always that way though. When Paul first became a member of the class, he had conflicts with other students. Paul would never forget the first class session. He was sitting beside a kid named Travis. Travis was a popular guy who attracted the attention of most of the girls in the class. Paul decided that he wanted attention too. He wanted to impress a pretty girl sitting directly across from him. He picked up his Dr. Pepper, took a long drink, and let out a loud, raunchy belch. Tammy gave Paul attention, but not the kind of attention he wanted.

Paul was not surprised when the kids in the class began to call him names and yelled at him to get out. This was the reaction Paul got most days. He hung his head and felt like crawling out of the room. How stupid could he be?

What Paul heard next nearly blew him away. Mr. Spencer's voice rose above the ridicule of Paul's classmates. He asked the students to be quiet and then told a story of how he had interrupted a class in a similar way when he was a teen. He explained how embarrassed he was and that it could happen to anyone. He told Paul he was sorry that he had been made fun of and that he shouldn't feel stupid for what he did. Paul wasn't sure if Mr. Spencer knew he had burped on purpose, but he felt good that he had been given a chance to redeem himself in front of this new group of kids. He was sure he would never have a great chance to date Tammy, but he could at least come back to class another day.

After class, Mr. Spencer approached Paul and asked him where he went to school and what he liked to do for fun. He invited him to join the Sunday School class after church that evening at the local burger place. He encouraged Paul to come back to class next week. Not once did Mr. Spencer bring up Paul's rude disturbance. This was different from anything Paul had ever experienced before.

Over the next few months, Paul made an effort to be around Mr. Spencer as often as possible. He would do things from time to time to try to cause Mr. Spencer to reject him, but each time his teacher would dwell on something positive Paul had done. After a while, Paul determined that Mr. Spencer actually liked him and understood him.

As Paul's trust of Mr. Spencer grew, he felt more free to talk to him. Mr. Spencer didn't approve of the things that Paul did, but he was always there to pray with him and to encourage him to do better. Mr. Spencer had given Paul hope when everyone else had given up on him. Since spending time with Mr. Spencer and being in his class, Paul thought that his behavior had improved. That's why this trip to the office had come as a shock.

Mrs. Zinn's voice broke the tension-filled silence. "Mr. Smith is ready to see you." Paul tried to detect what Mr. Smith wanted by the tone of Mrs. Zinn's voice, but her professional manner provided no hint of what was to follow.

Paul slowly shuffled into the office and took a seat in front of Mr. Smith's long, brown desk. Mr. Smith finished signing some papers and handed them to Mrs. Zinn. Once she left, Mr. Smith got up from his chair and walked toward Paul.

Paul's mind whirled as he tried to figure out what was going on. He felt the palms of his hands getting wet and rubbed them against his jeans. He wanted to get up and run as fast and as far as he could. The only thing that kept him in his chair was his memory of the words that Mr. Spencer had told him a few days ago, "No matter what the situation, God is there with you to give you help."

Mr. Smith's smile was the first sign that this office visit might be different from any that Paul had experienced before. Mr. Smith complimented Paul on his recent behavior. He said that Paul's teachers had noted his improved behavior over the last few months. Mr. Smith apologized for some of his earlier predictions and encouraged him to keep up the good work. He also told Paul that he had just signed a letter that was going to be placed in his school file that noted the great improvements he had made. Mr. Smith was sure that Paul's parents would be happy when they got their copy of the letter.

Paul left the office with a grin he couldn't quite control. He could hardly wait until he got home tonight. The first thing he was going to do was call Mr. Spencer and tell him what had happened.

6

They want answers.

"The Church cannot be content to live in its stain-glass house and throw stones through the picture window of modern culture."

Robert McAfee Brown

Nicodemus stroked his beard in his usual way. He wanted to be sure no one could read his thoughts. These late-night meetings of the ruling council had always made him uncomfortable. *Why couldn't the Council be more open? Could the city's authorities on righteousness gather under the cloak of darkness without creating suspicion? Surely those who questioned their integrity would have fresh ammunition when gossip of another meeting reached the people.* No, he had never cared for such meetings.

The topic of tonight's meeting only added to his discomfort. The usual plots to manipulate Roman authority, skim from the temple tax, or creatively swindle some unsuspecting family of their inheritance weren't on the agenda. Tonight's topic of discussion was even more frightening for Nicodemus—what to do with Jesus of Nazareth.

Nicodemus listened halfheartedly to the ranting of one of the younger Pharisees. Nicodemus knew the man was little more than a wanna-be—a young Politician skilled in saying just the right thing to the right people for his own benefit. Nicodemus feigned interest only to avoid suspicion, but his mind drifted to his own opinion of Jesus, uncertain though it was.

Nicodemus could name nearly a dozen teachers and rabbis who had caused them concern during his years on the Council. It seemed there was always someone with better answers, someone promising to end Roman rule. The Council had become quite skilled at going along with the ideas until the upstart was of no value to them and then siding with Rome's squelching of the rebellion. They could do it in their sleep, and with these late-night meetings it sometimes seemed as though they did.

The tension in the room made it clear that this Jesus was a greater challenge. He had made no threats toward Rome. Rather, He talked about a kingdom not of this world. The idea seemed ludicrous to all of them, but the thousands already following Him were a major threat. In just a matter of months, Jesus had risen to become the most popular teacher in the region—even more popular than the superstars on the Council.

That's their real motive, Nicodemus thought as he watched a new speaker offer his version of the same epithets and accusations. *They are jealous because the people are following after Him.* Nicodemus wanted to smile, but he stroked his beard inconspicuously instead.

Of course, the fact that Jesus had begun attacking the Pharisees and their righteousness added to their anger toward Him. Jesus had accused them of self-centeredness, wicked intentions, and more things that Nicodemus knew were true. And that's what made him uncomfortable on this night—and every other time that Jesus' name was mentioned. Jesus knew them. He knew their hearts. It was almost as if He was . . .

Nicodemus shook himself from his thoughts, unwilling to finish the statement even to himself. But the evidence was mounting. There was no explaining the miracles other than to conclude that Jesus had come from God. The lame were walking, the blind now read from the Torah, and the lepers were among the first to the synagogue, their skin smooth and whole.

And His teaching . . . there was nothing usual in His teaching. He spoke of God as though He knew Him . . . personally. He called God "Father" and described Him in ways Nicodemus wanted to believe, but was afraid to. There was simply no one like Him.

The volume of discussion was growing, but one couldn't help noticing that the older, well-advised members of the Council had remained silent. They had left the parade of accusations to the younger men whose objective was to make a name for themselves.

Finally, a senior member spoke softly, but with authority. "There is nothing to be done at this time."

The accusing men blanched, their faces contorting in disagreement, but most were afraid to speak. "Sir, shall we allow the entire nation to follow after Him?" one brave person ventured.

"The crowds are already too large," another Council leader spoke. "A move against Him will most likely backfire on us."

"He claims to be the Messiah!" another man shouted.

The first of the elders to speak stood slowly "Gentlemen, that is merely a rumor at this point. It is what the people believe, but according to our sources, He has yet to make such a claim for himself. Until He does, no charge of blasphemy will be leveled."

Nicodemus nodded. He hoped such words could be the first step toward a serious evaluation of what Jesus was teaching. After all, if he was the Messiah, shouldn't they be the first to recognize it? If the Council members could just calm down and discuss this intelligently, they might find some answers.

Nicodemus leaned forward, grasping the rail before him as he prepared to stand. But another man had already leaped to his feet. "What of His accusations against us? He must be silenced." His tone brought shouts of agreement from throughout the room. Nicodemus slumped silently back into his chair. There would be no intelligent debate tonight.

Finally, the head of the Council waved his hand for silence. Nicodemus knew what would come next. "Members of the Council," the old priest raised his voice, trying to present a dignity Nicodemus knew had long since parted. "This Jesus must be dealt with, but in time. Soon enough He will show His colors. He'll make a mistake, and the issue will be easily settled. We'll watch Him closely until He falls into our hands." The priest sat down. He smiled slightly, clearly satisfied with his power in such moments.

"And if He doesn't?" Nicodemus hadn't planned to speak, but his deep voice echoed clearly through the room with the question nagging most of them.

"Then we'll handle things our way." The words dripped with evil intent.

Nicodemus' eyes fell. He would not look into the wicked heart of his leader. This was wrong. So many times he had looked the other way, content to hold his position of authority and prestige. But this was too much. They needed answers . . . He needed answers! And if he couldn't get them here, . . . well . . . he'd find them for himself.

Nicodemus ignored the pockets of gossip that had gathered throughout the room and stepped out into the night. It was late, but maybe not too late to get some answers. Perhaps by morning he could get some, if not for the Council, then at least for himself.

**W**hy?"

If you've spent much time around a preschooler, you've heard the question before. "Why?" For the curious child, the question fits hundreds of encounters, circumstances, and explanations ad nauseam. A child's thirst for knowledge and the perceived need to accumulate it can drive a harried parent to the brink. Of course, the wise parent patiently provides the knowledge, grateful to be his child's link to the answers needed.

As we grow older, our need for answers doesn't diminish. We may become more adept at asking, but we still need answers, and, the questions get harder.

Why can't people get along? Why is my marriage failing? Why do so many good people die so young? Why doesn't God stop the violence? Why should I go on?

Of course, not every important question starts with *why*. We also need to know *how*. How can I succeed? How can I be a better parent? How can I protect my kids? How can I make a difference at work? How can I have a stronger marriage? How can I have the life I want?

It is the presence of these questions and thousands more just like them that underscore our need for answers. Perhaps the more important question is, "Where do we go to find the answers?"

For decades the Church has rallied under the idea that Jesus is the Answer. Indeed, we know that everything that searching people need can be found in the eternal truth of God's Word. But are people looking there?

Researcher George Barna, notes that "It is amazing that we live in a period during which people are more interested in spirituality than at any time in the past half century, yet they are seeking the answers to their spiritual questions and needs from sources other than Christian churches. The American public is sending a clear message to Christian leaders: make Christianity accessible and practical or don't expect their participation."[1]

People want answers. Actually, they're desperate for answers. Can they find them through the ministry of your church?

Perhaps the answer can be found in what we believe about God's Word. If your Sunday School class or small group studies the Bible simply to know the facts or master the content, then something may well be missing. Knowing the Bible as one might know Shakespeare has value, but there's a greater target than mere intellectual mastery. Every story, every statement, every principle contained in the Bible offers real answers for real people in every generation. God's Word offers the moral compass, the standard for living, the answer to life's most practical and fundamental questions. It is a book not just to be merely known or studied, but to be lived.

The pursuit of answers motivates most of the people in our communities. Although some of those questions are bigger than we are, we know the One who has those answers.

MAKING IT HAPPEN

Teachers generally come to class with predetermined agendas. They have studied the curriculum or developed their own lesson based on what they think their students need. As they walk through the classroom door, they are focused on getting the lesson objective across to their students. What they may fail to understand is that the students often arrive in class with their own agendas. A breakdown occurs when a teacher regularly offers answers to questions that the students are not asking.

A challenge faced by Christian educators is to find a balance between completing a prescribed course of study and providing timely responses to the immediate needs of their students. Here are a few suggestions that will help teachers find that balance.

EMBRACE THE NEED

A commitment to assist students in the discovery of biblical answers to contemporary questions will require teachers to adopt the following basic attitudes.

1. Be willing to entertain the tough questions.

Many teachers seek to avoid confronting the tough questions of life. It is much easier to talk about Adam and Eve's sin than it is to address the various ways Christians live in disobedience to God today. It is tempting to focus on the miracles of Jesus, while failing to address the question of why a child's parents got a divorce or why a wife was stricken with a disease that resulted in her death. When teachers present the biblical account without reconciling it with the realities students face daily, the Bible may seem irrelevant.

It takes courage to grapple with the tough questions of life, especially when the Bible doesn't provide clear-cut answers. Our inability to respond to every question shouldn't become an excuse to avoid tough questions. Remember that our failure to entertain tough questions in class does not prevent the questions from being asked in the minds of the students. Trust that the Bible contains principles that will apply to the issues at hand and commit yourself to study and pray with your students to find the answers that seem to be hidden from them.

2. View questions as opportunities rather than interruptions.

Questions that cause us to detour from our well-polished script can be a cause of irritation to some teachers. We don't mind so much when the question is anticipated and leads us to our next point, but seemingly off-the-wall questions often make us terribly uncomfortable.

If we want to meet the needs of those who attend our classes, we must adopt the mentality that questions are opportunities to minister to the needs of people rather than interruptions to our well-laid plans. When students make themselves vulnerable enough to ask a tough question, it is our responsibility to take that question seriously. There may be a more appropriate time to address the question than in the middle of a lesson, but some time must be given either during or after class where the teacher provides assistance in discovering God's answer to the student's query.

3. Recognize the ultimate purpose of Christian education.

The ultimate purpose of Christian education is not to present a lesson or to instill biblical facts in the memory of our students. The ultimate purpose of Christian education is to help individuals develop their faith so they can successfully serve God and their fellow human beings. The teacher must accept the responsibility of knowing when to adjust the lesson plan to help guide an individual or group toward Christ's solution to a unique problem.

ENHANCE THE ENVIRONMENT

Both teachers and students are frustrated when a teacher recognizes the need to encourage questions but fails to provide an environment that is inquiry friendly. Here are a few ideas that will help set the tone for exciting and effective interchange.

1. Become a facilitator of discovery.

No matter how intelligent you are, there is more value in accumulated wisdom than in your insights as a single individual. Avoid assuming the role of "answer man" by acting as a facilitator who draws information and solutions from the larger body of knowledge resident in the classroom. It is important to recognize the multiplied years of experience of those in the room whether you are teaching young people or adults. Help students help one another discover the truths in God's Word that relate to the problems they face.

2. Encourage student interaction.

An enemy to many teachers is silence. We have a tendency to become uncomfortable when we ask a question, and no one responds. Typically, we fill the silence with our own voices in an attempt to alleviate the awkwardness. As long as we follow this pattern, discussion will either be non-existent or controlled by the few who love to express their opinions.

Make an effort to encourage student interaction through the use of a variety of methods including discussion pairs, small group interaction, and the policy that prohibits domination by one or two people. Allow "thinking time" when you ask a question or seek insight from students.

3. Create a sense of mutual respect.

Probably the most important thing that you can do to create an environment that will be conducive to having questions asked and answered is to provide an environment of respect for each other. The old adage that there are "no dumb questions" must be reinforced continually. Classrooms that are characterized by a feeling of mutual respect will result in a healthy interchange of thoughts and exploration of biblical principles.

ESTABLISH THE STRATEGY

The Christian education classroom can house an exciting learning experience when teachers employ the right strategy. Here are a few components of a strategy that will allow this to happen.

1. Insist on relevance.

Above all else, strive for relevance. The day of students coming to class out of habit or obligation is soon to become extinct. Truth must be presented in such a way as to correlate with students' lives and concerns, or students will pay little attention to the message being presented.

2. Be familiar with the issues.

Many of the questions that students want answered are common to all age groups. Samples of these include "Who is God, and what does He say about himself?" "What is right or how should I live?" "Does loving others mean tolerating their belief systems and conduct?" and "What does the future hold?" All teachers must be ready to offer help for these questions.

In addition to these general-interest questions, each age group has its own set of issues. Children may ask why God allowed their pet to die. Teens may ask how premarital sex can be wrong if they love their partner. Adult issues range from family concerns to health issues. These are just a few of the questions being asked by those in your classrooms. Take the time to get to know your students and their situations. This will help you tailor your lesson in a fashion that will address questions the students are asking.

3. Concentrate on biblical principles.

Learning biblical facts can be fascinating, but this cannot be the total focus of a Sunday School class. Instead of simply focusing on the history of the Bible, always look for the timeless principle that is being communicated by the text. Most of today's questions can be answered by applying scriptural principles because the basic nature of man hasn't changed over time.

4. Capitalize on teachable moments.

A teachable moment is a point in time when a student is ready to listen and learn. In some cases, teachers communicate God's Word to people for years and can't seem to get through to them, but an event will arise that forces the students to want answers. At that moment, the Word will penetrate their heads and their hearts. Don't let those rare moments slip by without capitalizing on them. You can always return to your outline; you may never again have a similar opportunity to impact your students with God's Word.

5. Acknowledge your limits.

Don't pretend to have all the answers. Point students to the Word of God. People do not expect you to have all the answers. They are looking for authenticity in leaders who are a little farther down the road, but still learning and growing themselves.

ENGAGE THE STUDENT

The educational process is not complete until change has taken place in the student. Here are a few ways to facilitate that process.

1. Go beyond the "should."

Help your students realize that "I should" responses are mental responses that do little to change themselves or their world. Students who seek answers to their questions must be willing to apply the principles they learn. Those who fail to do so are not true seekers of answers; they are just trying to excuse their behavior or the behavior of others. Remind your students that they will be judged by what they do with the Word of God, not by the amount of scriptural knowledge they have obtained.

2. Empower your students.

When questions are asked in class, encourage other students to draw from their experience and knowledge base. If satisfactory answers are not forthcoming, assign students to come up with biblical responses in the coming week. Set expectations that all class members will be equal participants in the learning process.

3. Direct students to other resources.

Develop a list of resources that you can direct your students to in order to find answers. This list should include human resources as well as printed and recorded materials. The Internet provides many resources through various websites that have been developed to distribute biblical information. Encourage students to bring information back to class to share with fellow seekers.

Students come to class from a variety of backgrounds and bring baggage filled with accumulated hurts and joys from their individual journeys. Attempting to fit each of these uniquely formed individuals into prefabricated boxes makes the task of teaching easier, but it fails to address the needs of those who have come to class to hear practical answers from God's Word that will meet their needs. Make the effort to present the Scriptures in a manner that is faithful to the text and applicable to those who struggle with the realities of the twenty-first century.

IT'S HAPPENING

First Assembly of God located in Griffin, Georgia, is a place where people are able to explore the tough issues of life. An interview with Associate Pastor Tim Newby revealed some of the ways Sunday School has been used to minister to those who are searching for biblical answers to contemporary problems.

Pastor Newby believes that the church is responsible to address the issues of society because our world has abandoned the idea of absolute truth. As a result, people are left with multiple questions and have nowhere to turn to find answers if the church fails to actively respond.

The leadership at Griffin First Assembly acknowledges that their congregation benefits when it seeks to provide answers to the tough questions people ask. Newby states, "Our Sunday School classes have benefited greatly by approaching different topics that relate to life's tough questions. Not only have we seen numerical growth, but also spiritual growth in individuals and couples."

Griffin First Assembly uses a variety of methods to address the questions people ask. The church offers single and single-again classes that address questions specifically pertinent to that segment of society. Marriage and family classes provide answers to questions that plague our society. Extension classes are offered that meet on various nights of the week. Newby states, "We have helped people in the area of life-controlling problems with Weigh Down workshops, and reached out to our community and to those who are going through divorce with Divorce Care." The church is currently considering the addition of a class called Boundaries, which is designed to help people find balance in the key areas of their lives.

The church has an intentional approach to addressing tough issues for young adults and youth. Under the direction of the youth pastor, Tim Bach, the young people come into class and are introduced to a life application Bible subject and then enter into discussion groups of six to eight people. The leaders of each of these small groups meet regularly with the youth pastor for mentoring. This approach has allowed students the freedom to confront tough questions in a safe and healthy environment.

Griffin First Assembly's efforts to provide life's answers have had tangible benefits. One example is the transformation that has taken place in Myron's life. Myron is a divorced man who became acquainted with the church through its single and single-again ministry. After attending the Divorce Care group on Wednesday nights, he began to come to church services and found his way into the adult singles Sunday School class. Not long after becoming involved in the church, his son died of heart failure. Questions concerning his divorce and the reasons for the death of his son filled his mind. Myron found support and was allowed to explore his questions in his Sunday School class. Many years later, Myron now is the teacher of the singles class and coordinator for all adult singles activities of the church.

When asked for hints that he could share with other churches who want to do a better job of providing relevant answers, Pastor Newby states, "Find a need and meet it." He goes on to say, "People are coming to church from all walks of life, and there are people in our neighborhoods and cities who need answers. We have the answers through our relationship with God through Jesus Christ."

Newby provides these practical steps to becoming effective in this area. First he says, "When you see a 'need' in your church, put the 'need' to prayer, pray for the right person to step forward to teach a class or lead a small group so that discipleship and growth can be offered not only to those in your church, but also to those in your community." Next he suggests that you advertise in your community newspaper that you are offering life-answering classes. Third, he reminds you that there are countless people in your church who have come through life's tough issues, and they are valuable resources for sharing with others the keys for finding hope in the real world. Finally, he instructs you to always use the Word of God, because it alone provides the true answers. He concludes with this statement, "We are the Church, and we have the answer; it is a vibrant, life-changing relationship with Jesus Christ. It is through Him and His Word that answers will come to life's tough questions."

A FINAL LOOK

Bill sat on the edge of his bed slowly tying his shoe. It was Tuesday night, and that meant he would spend the evening at a local restaurant talking with his friend Dave. This had been an ongoing appointment on Bill's calendar for over a year now. There were times when Bill would have rather sat at home watching television, but he knew that what he was about to do was extremely important to the spiritual development of his friend.

Bill had met Dave a little more than sixteen months before, when Bill responded to a call for assistance from his pastor. Bill was an elder in his church and was often called on to assist in various ways. On this occasion Bill's pastor asked him to go to the hospital to minister to an unchurched family that had called the church requesting prayer. He was told that there was a woman there who had just that day been diagnosed with a terminal illness and that she wished to recommit her life to Jesus.

When Bill got to the hospital, he found a desperate woman. The unexpected diagnosis and the prospect of spending eternity in hell frightened her. She grabbed Bill's hand and told him how she used to attend church and worship God every week when she was a teen. She said that she had fallen away from God over the last few years. She wept bitterly in remorse for the pain she had caused her Savior. Bill was able to lead her in a prayer of recommitment and offered her renewed hope.

Dave stood at a distance and watched all of this. He was hurt and confused by the news of the day. He was not in the frame of mind to make any life-changing decisions, but if this was what his wife wanted, it was fine. Dave did not have a previous faith history to draw from as his dying wife did.

In her final days, Dave's wife began to tell him about the wonderful life she would soon be experiencing after her death. After she died, he began to rethink his own spiritual condition. He had loved his wife and wanted to share eternity with her. He was not sure about God in general or Christianity specifically, but he was willing to give anything a try to be with his beloved wife again someday. Dave called the only person he knew who could help him make that possibility a reality. Bill readily responded to Dave's request. That very week Bill and Dave got together and Dave accepted Jesus as his Savior.

Although Dave exercised faith in Jesus, he was not of the nature to accept the claims of Christianity without question. Dave had a lot of deep and heartfelt questions for which he wanted answers. Probably the most important question Dave had concerned God's love. He wanted to know how a loving God could steal his wife away from him. In conjunction with this, Dave wondered why an all-powerful God didn't respond to his or his wife's prayers for healing. Was this God too weak to do this? Or was He just too busy to be bothered by their situation? Neither of these options was extremely attractive to Dave. He wondered if there was any use in praying if God didn't readily respond to those prayers.

Dave had other more basic questions as well. He asked such questions as, "Why do Christians think their religion is superior to Buddhism, Hinduism, or any other belief systems held by people?" One night Dave asked, "Why do Christians feel it is necessary to sing hymns and give money to the church?" These are just samples of the questions Bill was confronted with each week from Dave.

Attempting to answer Dave's honest questions was one of the most difficult ministry tasks Bill had ever faced. If Bill had thought that Dave was playing games or just being argumentative, he would have stopped meeting with him long before now. But this was not the case. Dave was committed to serving God, but he had legitimate questions concerning the Christian faith and life in general. Bill was convinced that there was no question too difficult for God and His Word. It was Bill's desire to search the Scriptures with Dave and to seek God in order to discover the answers that he sought. As long as Dave was willing to participate in the discovery process, Bill was willing to walk along beside him, helping him to find his way.

Each week as Bill prepared to sit across from Dave, he would review the questions of the previous week and try to anticipate additional questions that might spring from these. He would then pray for guidance and wisdom from God to enable him to speak the words that would bring enlightenment and clarity. He would also request patience. He knew that he had a tendency to get frustrated when Dave demanded clear-cut answers to questions that were a matter of faith. It was especially in those times that Bill needed God to give him words and illustrations that would help Dave understand.

Bill thought back over the many hours that he had spent with Dave over the last year. As he reflected on the various questions asked, he was thankful that God had been faithful to respond to his prayers for help. No, Bill had not always had answers that satisfied Dave, but each night as they got into their respective automobiles and drove off, Bill knew that Dave had taken one step farther in his goal to understand the faith he had embraced and the God he now served.

Tonight after Bill tied his shoes and put on his coat, he walked out of his house thanking God for people like Dave. Not everyone who comes to faith in Jesus dares to ask such tough questions, but Bill was sure that almost everyone has questions for which they wished they had answers. Bill was glad he was part of a church that had answered his questions when he first became a Christian many years before.

Bill turned the key in the ignition and smiled contentedly. There wasn't a show on television good enough to keep him from spending the next couple of hours seeking answers to the perplexities of life with his good friend Dave.

 **ENDNOTE**

[1]Barna Research Group, Ltd. (1999). *One out of three adults is now unchurched,* [Online]. Available FTP: ww.barna.org

7

They want to learn a better way to live.

"Keep your feet on the ground, but let your heart soar as high as it will. Refuse to be average or to surrender to the chill of your spiritual environment."

A. W. Tozer

Levi, the others, they were right. Tears pressed hard against his eyelids until he could not hold them back. They had all been right. Zaccheus' face fell into his hands as he fought the emotion no longer.

In that moment the events of a lifetime pressed like a tidal wave through his mind. He had been the son of a poor man, a father who seemed never to find a way to care for his family. Zaccheus had often fought the urge to despise his father. Times had been hard for all families in Jericho. Life under the domination of Rome was seldom fair. Survival was the best most could achieve, and Zaccheus' father had achieved that. But it wasn't enough for Zaccheus. Before the age of eleven, he determined life wouldn't be that way for him, no matter what it cost.

Rome was his answer. He'd seen those in his village who worked with the Romans. His father called them traitors, but Zaccheus saw how those same people lived in the nicest homes and never lacked for food. That was the life he wanted. He wanted to be a friend to Rome.

At first it was the soldiers. Other boys would throw small stones or shout names at the Roman soldiers. Not Zaccheus. He was quick to make friends with these men, even helping them discover which boys had attacked them. Soon he was a regular at the homes of officials and finally landed an appointment as an apprentice to a tax collector.

Zaccheus knew his father would never approve. In a few weeks their relationship crumbled beyond repair. Their final words to one another were cruel. Zaccheus insisted crudely that he would give his family what his father never could. His father's eyes were filled more with hurt than anger as he banished his Roman son from their home.

If one could be a good tax collector, Zaccheus became one. In a few short years, he had risen above his peers in responsibility and wealth. His territory spanned nearly the entire region around Jericho where he could skim from the excess charged by a host of deputies. For three years now he had lived in the home of his dreams, and the plans for a larger place were nearly complete. If not for the suspicions of Rome, he might have already built it.

Every day Zaccheus carried more coins in his pocket than his father had held in a lifetime. He lacked for nothing. In fact, Zaccheus often wondered if there was any man in Jericho with more money. He might never know, since too public a display of his wealth might raise more suspicion. Just knowing that the amount buried beneath his home likely made his property the most valuable in the region would have to satisy his pride.

But money wasn't everything, and Zaccheus knew it. He had realized his dream, filled his life with every luxury, and proved his father a failure. Somehow, it wasn't enough. Deep within, feelings of dissatisfaction had begun to grow, feelings that even a foreclosure for non-payment of taxes could not soothe.

It was about the time that those feelings began when word came that Levi had abandoned a lucrative post up north to follow after a country teacher. Zaccheus had cursed Levi's foolishness and immediately dispatched an assistant to try to get a piece of Levi's estate. Over the next several months, word came of colleague after colleague who had made the same decision. With the departure of each friend, a bit of Zaccheus' scorn turned to curiosity.

Today had started with the news that this country teacher who had pried so many of Rome's finest from their wealthy service was coming to Jericho. Zaccheus had fought hard to hold back his interest. He wanted to dismiss the foolishness of the others, but that nagging dissatisfaction prevented it. *Maybe if I just saw Him . . . to see what the fuss is all about,* he decided. *Not too close, just a face in the crowd. That would be enough,* he had reasoned.

But Zaccheus hadn't anticipated the size of the crowd. Not a tall man, another demeaning legacy of his father, Zaccheus quickly recognized that a place in the front was the only way he'd get a clear view of this Jesus. But then his curiosity would be too obvious. There had to be another way . . . and there was. Within seconds, the region's wealthiest, and probably most hated, man had scurried up a tree, demanding silence of the three boys who had already selected the perch. They sat wide-eyed, nearly as stunned by his impulsiveness as he was himself. But there was no time for another plan; Jesus was already in view.

The events of that momentous day happened so fast that Zaccheus could hardly recall them clearly. He remembered only that Jesus had spotted him, called him by name, and asked to spend the day with him. After a few stammering commands to a servant, a meal had been prepared. It was here they had sat . . . for the past several hours.

They were right, he thought again. Those he had scorned as foolish now looked bright in their wisdom. Zaccheus' shoulders shook with sobs as a love he never knew existed flowed from the words of this man. The pain, the competitiveness, even the anger he still held toward his father washed from his heart in the flood of tears. Nothing had ever made him feel such guilt and such . . . peace. If only . . .

His father had been dead two years now, and it had been months since he'd been to the home of his youth even though it stood only a few streets from his palace. If only . . .

"Look, Lord!" Zaccheus sobbed. "Here and now I give half of my possessions to the poor . . ."

Jesus' face didn't change. It was an expression of wonder and love, like a child watching a butterfly emerge from its cocoon.

"If I cheated anyone out of anything, I will pay back four times the amount," Zaccheus exclaimed.

Jesus said nothing. He placed his hand on Zaccheus' shoulder and stood to leave. Zaccheus embraced Him once more before the country teacher stepped back into the street and into the crowd that waited. The small man followed for a few steps, then stopped and turned to the curious faces surrounding him. In that moment he realized that Jesus hadn't demanded any payment or placed any price on the peace that now filled Zaccheus' heart. Jesus just showed him a better way to live.

Without hesitation Zaccheus announced his plans to all who would listen. He would give money back as he had promised Jesus. There was much he needed to do. Smiling, he wondered what his colleagues in Jerusalem would say of him now.

$\mathcal{T}$he Spirit of the Lord is on me, because he has anointed me to preach good news to the poor. He has sent me to proclaim freedom for the prisoners and recovery of sight for the blind, to release the oppressed, to proclaim the year of the Lord's favor" (Luke 4:18–19).

With these words Jesus launched the three most significant years of ministry in the history of our world. His announcement, a direct quote from the prophet Isaiah, unveiled new hope for His audience and every life lived since. The promises in these words reveal an enhancement both of life's quality and its quantity for all time. In another setting He confirmed that He had come to give life to the full to those who would trust in Him.

There's not a person in your community who doesn't need it. There aren't sufficient pages in this text to list the stresses of our day. Anxiety and uncertainty are growing in common experience, outpacing death and taxes at least in frequency. While in North America the standard of living exceeds that of virtually every corner of the earth, most people know the difference between standard of living and quality of life.

It was once thought that technological advances would increase leisure time for many of us. By now we know that the opposite has occurred. The ability to accomplish more has bred the expectation to accomplish more. Technology has accelerated both the pace of life and the demands for better performance. Peace is a distant dream, more likely achieved in moments of escape than consistently experienced in daily living.

Money hasn't done the trick either. According to Forbes magazine, more than five million Americans have a net worth of at least one million dollars. That's nearly triple the number just ten years ago. In the recently strong economy, personal income has surged for thousands, leaving us with greater financial resources than ever before. But have fulfillment and satisfaction risen correspondingly? Probably not.

Many Americans are searching for a better way to live. They have faced the disappointment and defeat of lifestyles poorly chosen. Now they live in fear, unprepared for the anxieties of life in a culture that is increasingly violent. Some have climbed to the top of the mountain only to find their success barren and lonely. Others keep climbing, resisting the growing knowledge of the dissatisfied experiences of thousands of previous climbers. They want a better life, but they are reluctant to stop climbing. They don't want to believe that worldly success is not the better life.

What a marvelous opportunity for Jesus, for the truth, and for your Sunday School class! Christ did come and bring a better way to live, a way that is founded on eternal principles and truth. That's what people want, and they're liable to come your way looking for it. Are you ready for them? Are you ready to unveil the path of grace and righteousness to those who are seaching?

They want a better way to live—and you've got it!

MAKING IT HAPPEN

In the first eleven verses of John chapter eight, the apostle records a most startling story. A woman, caught in the act of adultery, finds herself suddenly leaping from death row to new life. The story reveals the full work of the gospel—forgiveness, repentance, and new life—against the backdrop of a self-righteous and hateful world. It's a story that ought to thrill every Christian, for it displays the journey we each have experienced with Christ.

Can we promise such an experience to those mired on spiritual death row in our communities? The first part, extending God's grace, seems within our grasp. But, the "go and sin no more" new life still challenges even the most experienced Christian. Offering new life goes beyond helping people escape the old one. It is a new life, an abundant, satisfying life of joy that they seek. Can we give them what they want?

EMBRACE THE NEED

Many in our communities seem content with their existence. They scurry toward self-destruction, oblivious to their destination, masking any feelings of discomfort with the adrenaline rush of pleasure. Others live farther from the edge and seem confident that their daily performance is the most one can expect from this life. A new way of life is no priority for them. The deficiencies of their current lives have yet to surface and propel them toward change.

Some in our communities have discovered the dissatisfaction of life without God. They have uncovered the first sign of wisdom—the need for God. They are the ones who come seeking a better way to live. "I can't make it on my own," is their proclamation. And they are looking to you and your church to help chart a new course, one that will bring the kind of life they dream of.

135

1. Be an outpost of forgiveness.

The first step toward new life is the willing abandonment of the old life. The Bible promises that God will make us into new creations, but we must deal with the old in order to find such freedom. The first step to a better way of life is to seek and experience God's forgiveness for where we've been.

As a teacher, you are a key illustration of God's forgiveness. You, along with your pastor and others in your congregation, are a communicator of Christ's forgiveness. If we teach that Christ has removed our sin and given us new life, we must be equally willing to view the students through new eyes. Where they've been and what they've done has been cast away by the prayer of faith and repentance. The students and the Savior have moved on—so must we.

It can be difficult to view some new Christians through the eyes of Christ. Sometimes, we are even tempted to take a wait-and-see approach to determine if they have really changed. A teacher cannot afford such a posture. The students need direction on the new path, and they are seeking your help. As a teacher, you must acknowledge the power of God's grace for your students lives in order to believe it is real and see it in action.

2. Recognize your role.

There's more to Sunday School teaching than the challenge of surviving the hour or completing a lesson. Your students need to know how to live. They are seeking a compass to guide them, and you are in the prime position to offer such direction. Sunday School teachers who acknowledge this part of their ministry open themselves to a new insight and spiritual priority.

Are your lessons relevant? Do you help your students find the daily impact of the Bible's teaching? For most of your students, knowing the events of Moses' life doesn't satisfy without understanding the modern lessons to be applied. Simply put, you are teaching more than Bible content. You are teaching a way of life.

ENHANCE THE ENVIRONMENT

What can you do to establish an environment of life learning for your students? It may not be as difficult as it sounds. Consider these steps.

1. Cultivate love and understanding.

Condemnation of sin is a part of the Church's communication to this world, but a condemning attitude toward sinful people seldom reveals the love of Christ. Small groups where individuals feel safe acknowledging their struggles provide the best hope for life change.

Most sinful behavior results from deeper issues than what may be most easily seen. Loneliness and fear often motivate some people to do what everyone else is doing. Others have never had the kind of positive role model that leads to better choices. Still others are strangled by low self-worth, and destructive behavior simply follows. An atmosphere that acknowledges sin as a real struggle will help students find hope rather than just guilt.

2. Model your own story.

It's a simple thought, really. A class where the students know the teacher is "human" will give the students confidence and comfort. Share your own story, your victories, and even a few setbacks. After just a short while, many of your students will want to be like you or reflect qualities they see in you. Tell them what God has done and is doing in you. Describe the lessons you've learned and how you learned them and the choices you've made and why you made them. Your real-life example is the clearest road map to a new life you can offer.

3. Make forgiveness and repentance normal.

Building into your teaching and classroom experience frequent times of repentance for sin will help your students become comfortable with God's forgiveness.

4. Create expectation.

Announce your desire to help your students build quality lives. Let them know that your class is a "laboratory for life." Whet the students' appetite and expectation each week by consistently targeting strong application for daily living. Once this expectation is established, enthusiasm will skyrocket.

ESTABLISH THE STRATEGY

Building lives is hard work. And true life change is supernatural in nature. But there are specific strategies you can implement that will contribute to the process. Consider these possibilities.

1. Give opportunities.

If you want to see changed lives, you must give opportunities for change. Always provide the opportunity for students to respond to what they've learned. But be creative. Don't allow how they respond to become routine. Be certain that the response is tailored to the decision you want them to make. Plan and pray about where you want their response in the lesson and how you will encourage it.

2. Find a new family.

Often, students struggle to abandon old habits and sinful lifestyles because they haven't changed their circles of influence. Help your students find new friends who want to march toward new life with them. This is one of the greatest areas of potential for your class.

3. Help your students define their mission.

What are they looking for? God's direction? Better parenting skills? The ability to get along with a sibling? Fulfillment? Challenge your students to define what they're after. Young children will need your help, but even they can understand why we've come to Sunday School and what help we need to live God's way, showing love to one another.

4. Provide a specific faith.

Help students determine specific ways the truth translates to their lives at home, on the job, in their activities, etc. Teach them to be specific in applying truth with definite people, definite situations, and definite actions in mind. Students never have to deal with the cost of the deep demands of following Christ every day in every aspect of life if faith is obscured in generalities.

5. Be relevant.

Be sure your students see the relevance of your teaching to their daily living. You may want to offer special classes to address needs in your community. People want help with what is confronting them each day. If you meet them at that need, they'll see your class and your church as valuable and relevant for their lives.

6. Commit to principles.

Help your students by distilling every teaching session into a principle or two. Let them leave the class with a life principle tucked into their heart that will guide their decision making or attitude all week.

7. Use real-life illustrations.

If real life is what we're teaching, then real-life illustrations are the most effective. This doesn't mean there is little benefit to biblical or historical illustrations, but we need to be sure contemporary applications of those principles are central to the lesson.

8. Don't fear homework.

End every class period with a "life assignment" for the week. If you're teaching on love, challenge the students to show kindness to a difficult person in their lives during that week. Then give opportunity the following week for them to share the results. It may take a few weeks to build expectation and response, but if you're consistent, you'll see results.

ENGAGE THE STUDENT

Your students want the very best life they can find, and many are willing to admit that they can't find it on their own. Once they commit to God's way, the door is open for you to help guide them toward a new way of living. But it is their road! God's plan for their lives will be unique. Your goal is not to clone yourself, but to help your students find God's plan for their own lives.

1. The classroom altar.

We have alluded to this area frequently in this chapter, but the altar deserves much emphasis. Your students must have opportunity to meet with God, and you cannot assume they will get that opportunity elsewhere. Open the way for response to God's Word every time you study it together.

2. Meaningful involvement.

While the first step toward new life is the abandonment of the old one, there must be something to replace the old life. Help your students find new habits to cultivate and ways of getting involved in God's work. Class ministry projects geared at the spiritual development of your students can be a great outlet for the desire within them.

Many people are unhappy with their lives. Others feel overwhelmed by their responsibilities. The church that can identify and address these feelings possesses great appeal to the struggling. God has shown us a better way to live, and it is our privilege to offer it to every individual in our communities.

IT'S HAPPENING

Capital Christian Center located in Sacramento, California, is a church where people discover a better way to live. Tom Houghton, pastor in charge of discipleship ministries, provided information concerning the church's intentional approach to discipleship that makes this new life a reality.

Houghton points to Psalm 119:1–5 as a guiding force for the church's discipleship ministry. The leadership of Capital Christian Center want people to be blessed, and they believe the Scriptures teach that a primary avenue for blessing in a person's life is to walk according to God's standards.

Capital Christian Center has purposely developed ministries that foster healthy lifestyles. The focal ministry that accomplishes this is the Sunday School. According to Houghton, "Each child from nursery through elementary, middle school, and high school has the opportunity to learn of God's ways. A child is never too young to learn. College age and young marrieds have the opportunity to meet and study. . . . [we have classes for people] all the way through to our most senior members. This is the core of what we do."

In addition to Sunday School, Capital Christian Center offers a variety of intentional ministries that help shape people's lives. The "School of Parenting" attracts parents and soon-to-be parents in a small-group setting to learn parenting skills. Premarital sessions are required for all couples planning to get married. Mentors are established to walk the engaged couple through God's ways regarding marriage. "Marriage By The Book" provides married couples with an extensive investigation of what "The Book" has to say about marital relationships. The church offers a small group ministry based on Crown Ministry materials that help people become good stewards of God's money. It also offers estate planning opportunities for those who are interested. In addition to all of these ministries, Capital Christian Center offers classes designed to help those people who have become entangled in life-controlling situations.

Chris is an example of a person whose life has been changed through the ministries of Capital Christian Center. Chris attended the church from time to time with his wife and children. Several times Chris responded to an altar call, but each time he would eventually fall back into the habits and patterns established over a number of years. Two years ago, Chris responded again to the Lord. This time he and his wife started to participate in the weekly class for new believers. Over the course of the next year, Chris's life began to change. The changes at times seemed small, but the transformation was significant as he began to understand and apply what was discussed each week. Today Chris helps teach the fourth and fifth grade Crosstrainers each Wednesday. His wife Wendy teaches weekly in the children's ministry. According to Houghton, "their lives have been transformed by the grace of God."

When asked for suggestions for others who wish to implement an emphasis on changed lives in their local church, Houghton offered the following ideas. "Focus the teaching ministry on the Word of God. The Word contains the instruction we all need to walk in His way and be blessed in this life and in the life to come. The Holy Spirit will take the simplest of teaching presentations and make them applicable to each individual who receives it." Houghton went on to say, "Actively encourage people to participate in Sunday School. In our rapid-paced society, we are driven away from relationships, busy schedules barely allowing enough time for families or a few quiet minutes for ourselves. Sunday School is a great opportunity to build relationships with other believers. Proverbs 27:17 states, 'As iron sharpens iron, so one man sharpens another.' This sharpening can occur in Sunday School."

Capital Christian Center provides an example for all churches to follow. Sunday Schools and churches that intentionally shape people according to the principles of Scripture will be instruments of blessing and will be blessed by those who are being transformed into the image of Jesus.

A FINAL LOOK

Rhonda sat at the bar, slowly sipping her drink. It would simply be a matter of time before someone she had never met would sit down beside her, make some small talk, and offer to buy her a drink. If this night was like most of the others, she would end up getting drunk, staggering back to her apartment with her new friend, and waking up the next morning to find that he had left sometime during the night. The activities of this evening would simply add to the long list of meaningless encounters that were becoming a composite of her life. Rhonda knew that she was living dangerously, but she had been living like this for so long that she no longer thought much about the consequences of her actions.

Rhonda hadn't always lived in such a tragic fashion. When she was a child, most people figured that she would be a success at whatever she attempted. Her smile always brightened the room. The excitement she embodied earned her the title of "most popular" among her junior high classmates. She was involved in a host of activities and social events. Nothing then indicated that Rhonda's life would degenerate into a series of high-risk, dead-end relationships.

Rhonda's effervescence became her eventual downfall. Upon entering high school, Rhonda began to attract the attention of the upper classmen. At first it was exciting to be asked out by lots of good-looking seniors. But there was one special guy that she wanted to date. Jeff was the captain of the high school tennis team. He was tall, tanned, and talented. Rhonda began to arrange settings where Jeff could notice her. It worked, and before she knew it, she was dating Jeff seriously.

Jeff and Rhonda began to spend increasing amounts of time together. At first they dated with a small group of friends, but by the fifth week of their romance, they found themselves spending a great deal of time alone at Jeff's house. Rhonda dropped out of most of her school activities. Her parents were concerned, but Rhonda assured them that everything was all right.

March 18 was a pivotal date in Rhonda's life. It was on that day that she discovered that she was pregnant. She had mixed emotions. She was afraid of what her parents would say, but she was excited because she was sure that this would cement her relationship with Jeff. She began to fantasize about the happy life the three of them would share together as a family.

Rhonda decided to tell Jeff before she told her parents. She felt that it would be easier for them to tell her parents as a couple and to share their long-term plans with them. When Rhonda shared her exciting news with Jeff, her dream world was shattered. His immediate response was anger as he asked her if she was positive that she was pregnant. When she explained that she had gone to a clinic that afternoon and that there was no doubt that she was pregnant, he looked at her in disgust and asked if she was sure the baby was his. His angry and accusing response offended her, but not as much as his demand that she return to the clinic and abort the baby.

Rhonda was never the same after that day. Her relationship with Jeff evaporated, and what hope she had for a joyful life seemed to disappear. Her parents observed a dramatic change in Rhonda when she and Jeff broke up, but they thought that things would get better after she forgot Jeff and moved on with her life. What they didn't know, however, was the secret that haunted her day after day.

During Rhonda's sophomore year in high school, she began to sink into a deep depression. Her parents attempted to get her professional help, but she refused to respond. Instead she attempted to dull the pain of her life through alcohol, drugs, and meaningless illicit encounters. She vowed that she would never give her heart to another man. She determined that she would use them the way she had been used by Jeff. Rhonda began a lifestyle that followed her to this day. What little self-respect Rhonda still had was lost when she made her way a second time into the barren abortion clinic.

Rhonda felt the brush of someone sitting down beside her. She wondered if this would be the guy she would go home with tonight. It really didn't matter to her. She no longer felt shame or guilt about what she did. As a matter of fact, she didn't feel much of anything anymore.

The next time Rhonda awoke she was not in her own bedroom. She looked around herself and recognized the furnishings as those typically associated with a hospital. She wondered why she was here, but quickly determined it had something to do with the bandages that encompassed her face and the throbbing feeling that was coming from her back and side. A friendly nurse asked her how she was feeling. Rhonda wasn't sure how to respond.

Rhonda discovered that her latest barroom affair had turned violent. The guy she was with had led her out of the bar and into an alley. There he punched her and kicked her until she was unconscious. He left her bleeding on the cold, wet ground. Strangely, she didn't feel anger toward this man. She felt that she had probably gotten what she deserved. She wasn't worthy of a man who would treat her well.

Later that evening, Rhonda's mother slipped into the room. She took Rhonda's hand and silently prayed for her. Rhonda's eyes raised to meet her mother's, then dropped. Her mother whispered that she loved her and would continue to pray for her. When Rhonda refused to respond, her mother turned and left the room.

Rhonda couldn't go back to sleep right away. She began to think about how good life had once been and how awful it was now. She beat herself up emotionally as she thought about the destructive choices she had made. She wondered if there was any way out of the mess she had created for herself. Before drifting off to sleep, she offered a prayer in hopes that someone in heaven would hear her. "Dear God, please show me a better way to live."

8

They want truth.

"The best way to show that a stick is crooked is not to argue about it or to spend time denouncing it, but to lay a straight stick alongside it."

D.L. Moody

"I'm hungry," Simon sighed, his words barely audible above the din of the crowd. Matthew nodded with a bit of a grin. Both men knew it would be awhile before they ate.

The last few days had been unlike any the young zealot had ever experienced. When he had first joined those following this new teacher, Jesus, it had been more out of curiosity than commitment. This country preacher, as some called Him, had already created quite a stir. With no family, no responsibility, no real direction in his life, Simon had found himself free to follow along. *Maybe, just maybe, this is the one who'll lead the much needed rebellion against Rome,* Simon had thought.

But Simon had found Jesus to be an enigma. He didn't seem eager to go against Rome. Actually, He never encouraged rebellion at all. How could He ever lead them to create a Jewish kingdom? Simon shook his head thoughtfully. Yes, He was hard to figure out. He spoke about a kingdom, one not like any Simon had ever imagined. Some of His teaching seemed unrealistic. Still, there was something about the man that Simon wanted to trust. And Simon did trust Him. In just a few weeks, Simon's curiosity about Jesus turned to dedication to Him. Though there was so much yet to understand, Simon knew he wanted to be a part of this strange kingdom, and he would do what was necessary to make it happen.

To be included in the inner circle of Jesus' followers had been quite a surprise. Maybe it was because he had become so attached to Jesus or because he was so willing to listen and obey everything Jesus said. Simon didn't really know, and he had never asked Jesus why He chose him. But, he was determined to prove himself a devoted follower in whatever way necessary. These were incredible days in Israel, and following this man Jesus was the best place to be.

Dozens of people pushed passed Simon. Those who wanted to see Jesus moved one way while those He had touched now moved the other. Just watching was exhausting. And his stomach now frequently reminded Simon that there'd been no time for breakfast.

These people are so desperate, Simon thought. With all the noise Matthew probably wouldn't have heard him if he'd said it out loud anyway. And there was no point, really. They'd had the conversation about the crowds many times. Everywhere they went, people seemed to have no hope. They flocked to Jesus. It was as if they couldn't get enough teaching and healing and compassion from Him. Some clung to Him, others begged to see Him. Still more wanted to go with Him wherever He went. It was incredible! Oddly, Jesus seemed to have enough love for every one of them. Simon was still amazed even though the scene had become quite familiar.

But today hadn't been like other days. It started with their first meeting together since Jesus had sent the twelve of them out to the villages. Simon and Matthew were among the first to catch up with Jesus that morning, but soon the whole group had arrived. They were all excited to tell the incredible stories of what they'd experienced. Simon knew he and Matthew would never be the same after that trip, preaching what Jesus had told them.

The disciples' excitement had been interrupted with the report that John the Baptist was dead. The sadness in Jesus' eyes penetrated each of their hearts, but no one knew what to say. Then the crowds found them, and it had been chaos ever since. Yes, these were remarkable times.

The smell of bread brought a sudden change in Simon's thoughts.

Later that day Simon stood beside Matthew. They were surrounded by hundreds, no thousands, of people. Soon it would be dark, and the crowds had never gone away.

Around noon, Jesus had pulled His group together, saying He wanted to go by boat to a quiet place, but it was no use. They had gone in the boat, but the people raced around the shore, and the crowds were even larger when Simon brought the boat to the shore. "These people are desperate," Matthew had commented, and Simon nodded in agreement.

Simon scanned the crowd. The light of the sunset revealed what must have been thousands of people pressed together, still wanting to hear what Jesus was saying. Who could blame them? Simon had been with Jesus for months, and he couldn't get enough of the truth Jesus brought. He had feasted on Jesus' teaching every day. Now many of these people were tasting their first morsel. Every word, every thought Jesus spoke about the kingdom of God—the kingdom that He had brought to them—satisfied a deeper hunger than they had ever known.

And Jesus made God seem so . . . so different from anything they'd ever heard. He wasn't a god who blessed and cursed His people on a whim like some had taught. He wasn't a god who wanted people to depend on themselves or take matters into their own hands. Simon had heard that teaching from many of his former friends. Jesus described God as a Father, a loving Father who cared deeply for His wayward children, and a Shepherd who longed to recover and care for His sheep. Jesus' teaching about God was so different from the things most of them had been taught. It was not surprising that none of these thousands had moved a muscle in nearly four hours as they hung onto His words.

"You still hungry?" Matthew whispered, smiling. Simon returned the smile, realizing it had been hours since he'd thought about his own stomach. Andrew had already pulled the other disciples together, and their concerned faces probably meant they'd had the same thought. It was already late, and they were a long way from any food. Reluctantly, Simon drifted toward the others, but he kept his attention on Jesus, the one he willingly called Master.

Simon was hungry, but somehow food wasn't the most important thing on his mind. As he looked across the faces of those who stood with him, it was clear that none of them were thinking about bread either.

These people were hungry—they were hungry for truth.

hat is truth?"

Pilate's query of Christ seems an odd moment during the trial of our Savior. Jesus had affirmed His claim of deity with the words, "You are right in saying I am a king." Pilate's follow-up question is out of place. "What is truth?" It doesn't appear that he doubted the response of Jesus. Rather, he seemed overwhelmed by the falsehoods surrounding Jesus' trial, His city, perhaps his entire life. If Jesus' trial had been about truth, well . . .

But Pilate's seemingly cynical statement doesn't seem out of place in our culture. The very concept of truth or the idea that it exists is under steady attack. Webster's concept of "a judgment, proposition, or idea that is true or accepted to be true" is vanishing. In its place, truth is becoming defined more subjectively, more in a manner dependent on circumstances. The idea of absolute truth, that is, truth that transcends situations or personal preference, is sliding from western belief systems.

It is staggering to learn that the Church is struggling with this issue. The body of Christ, the very repository of eternal truth, has been snared by modern doubt. According to the Barna Research

Institute, "four out of every ten individuals currently involved in a Christian discipling process contend that there is no such thing as absolute moral truth." The report continues by pointing out, "There is a lot of good intent but serious theological confusion among Christians in our culture today."[1]

More research shows that only 50 percent of Christians say there are moral truths which are unchanging, or that truth is not relative to the circumstances.[2] While that is double the number of non-Christians, the data is appalling. Truth is taking a beating in the marketplace, and the impact on even the Church is staggering.

And yet, those who have abandoned truth aren't finding fulfillment in their freedom from the concrete. Though 16 percent of Americans report that whatever works in their life is the only truth that they know, most find the answer unsatisfying.[3] They still want truth.

Could it be that Pilate's cynical question was accompanied by eyes hungry for hope? More importantly, do the people of our postmodern era think that truth, no matter the discomfort it brings, actually might exist? If so, where will they look? The options are plentiful, but certainly any serious search for truth will include the Church on the itinerary. If truth exists, surely it can be found among God's people.

It may be that the desire for truth is not the hunger closest to the surface. The need for friends or the longing for fun may be felt first. But the poverty of one's soul will ultimately reach the surface. And in that moment, only truth will satisfy. It's truth they need, and, for many, it is truth they want.

MAKING IT HAPPEN

Biblical teaching in any ministry of the local church should be a given primacy. The fact is that some churches spend very little time exploring the Word of God. Various demands gobble up precious moments that originally were intended for Bible study. When this occurs, people walk away from church having experienced the worship of God and enjoyed fellowship, but they remain hungry because of a lack of spiritual food.

People come to church because they believe that the Bible provides unquestionable truth that they get in no other place. It is our responsibility as teachers of God's Word to faithfully confront our students with that truth each time we gather together.

EMBRACE THE NEED

At one time teachers could assume that all Christians accepted God's Word as unquestionable truth. This assumption can no longer be made. Today, even some Christian education teachers are willing to question the validity of God's Word. This should not be the case. It is important that you accept the following principles in your quest to present the truth to those you teach.

1. Believe that there is a source of truth.

Relativism is the basic philosophy of the postmodern age. If you have attended public schools since the early sixties, you are a product of relativistic thinking. This philosophy teaches that there are no absolutes. Truth is determined by the individual and can change as the situation changes. The idea that there is an individual document that contains truth is ridiculous to many in our world today. As a teacher of God's Word, it is essential that you reject this relativistic thinking and embrace the fact that the Bible is true regardless of the attacks that come against it in the name of tolerance. Only when you have embraced this fact will you be able to effectively declare the life-changing gospel of Jesus Christ.

2. Move beyond indoctrination.

The doctrines of our church are important for all people to understand from the very earliest years. Doctrine must be taught at the student's level of understanding. But it is important to teach the Scriptures from which these truths are derived as we ask students to memorize the doctrines of the church. In that way, the students gain a true understanding of the biblical meaning behind the doctrine. To avoid recitation of truth without true knowledge of the truth, always attempt to engage your students with the text of Scripture and then lead them to the truth that is contained therein. This is important in order for the students to make the truth their own.

3. Discover the truth personally.

Those who understand the importance of teaching the truth in class will be willing to spend the time necessary to discover truth personally. This means that they will discipline themselves in the skills of Bible study methodology. By doing so, they will avoid doctrinal errors that result from sloppy interpretation skills. It is crucial that those who claim to value the presentation of truth have the commitment to do the hard work involved in discovering the truth on an ongoing basis.

ENHANCE THE ENVIRONMENT

Set an expectation among your students that they will hear the Word of God each week and be expected to respond appropriately to it. Here are some ways to encourage your students and yourself to consistently engage in the discovery of truth.

1. Use your Bible each week.

As obvious as this may seem, many teachers unintentionally discourage their students from bringing their Bibles to class by not having them use them when they get there. Have your students read from their Bibles during class time. Create questions based on the text of Scripture so students have to interact with their Bibles and personally discover the meaning of the original writer. Students who rely on your interpretation of the text will get into the habit of being consumers rather than owners of truth.

2. Create an atmosphere of openness.

Don't be afraid of the differing viewpoints your students may present concerning the meaning of Bible passages. If the student is misguided theologically, kindly point out the error in his or her thinking. If the student brings out a point that you have not seen or that has not been highlighted in the curriculum, be bold enough to explore the possibility that the student has gained insight that you and/or the curriculum writer have missed. Discovering truth is not limited to the "experts." Greater insights are possible when more people are engaged in the learning process.

3. Don't be a know-it-all.

It is essential that you have done your homework before coming to class, but avoid coming across as the final authority regarding the Bible. Remember that the Bible is truth and in most cases can speak for itself. One teacher pointed out that 85 percent of the Bible's truth is clear enough for anyone to understand; 10 percent can be understood with the help of scholars and commentaries; and the other 5 percent will be a mystery until the arrival of Jesus. While some may debate his numbers, the point is valuable. Set an expectation that all your students can understand God's truth by concentrating on the 85 percent; help them to use Bible study tools to discover the 10 percent, and allow the 5 percent that is subject to debate remain a mystery, believing God to be faithful to reveal that truth as He sees fit.

ESTABLISH THE STRATEGY

The teaching of truth must be approached differently at the various age levels. Teens and adults have the ability to comprehend truth and its application. Although these groups may struggle with postmodern thinking, they are ready to grapple with its implications. Many children younger than seven or eight years find it difficult if not impossible to distinguish fantasy from facts, dreams from real events, or pretend from real life. Teachers must keep these differences in mind as they prepare their strategy for teaching truth. Here are a few general rules that will keep you on track at all age levels.

1. Insist on biblical interaction.

There is little that frustrates a serious student of the Word more than people who spend valuable classroom time expounding pet theories. It seems that every class has someone who is a seeming expert on every subject. These individuals often dominate the class discussion, and by the time the class session is over, little has been gained. It is vital that this pattern not be allowed to develop in your class. A key to preventing this situation, or for turning it around, is to continually refer students back to the Bible and its meaning. Kindly tell those who would like to share their theories that you are engaged in a Bible study, not a theology or philosophy class. Reinforce this by allowing the Bible to speak for itself and by taking the role of resource person, adding background information that illuminates the text and its meaning.

2. Focus on principles rather than cultural expressions.

An important consideration of biblical interpretation concerns the question of what details in the Bible applied solely to the period in which it was written and what still applies today. We do the Bible injustice to assume that everything it declares should continue to be practiced today. Few would think it would be appropriate to stone our children in a public square if they spoke ill against us.

Even though we reject the practice of throwing rocks at our children as punishment, we do not reject the principle that there should be consequences when children show disrespect to their parents. The how-to of the principle may change, but the principle never does. It is essential that we endeavor to discover truth principles and find appropriate cultural application.

3. Move from philosophy to faith.

The idea of truth is much more easily obtained than the practice of truth. Recognize that making truth an integral part of a person's life is a process that takes time. Reinforcing the truth in our words and actions will be more beneficial than condemning a person and giving up on the person's ability to ever accept truth to the point of practicing it. An uncompromised stance on biblical principles must be marked by evident compassion on the part of the teacher.

4. Engage in expository teaching.

Expository teaching is a systematic approach to teaching that takes students through the Word of God and allows it to speak to the various issues of life. It is helpful at times to search the Scriptures to find help or principles that deal with a particular issue, but this should not be the sole approach of any Bible study. God's truth must be studied within the context of the situation and the time of the writer and then applied to our lives. This is best done when we study it in the fashion it was written—a chapter-by-chapter, book-by-book exploration.

5. Acknowledge your limits.

Don't pretend to have all the answers. If you don't know the answer, say so. Challenge your students to dig deeper into the

Word, to search the resources available to them, and to come back and share with the class what they have discovered.

ENGAGE THE STUDENT

It is not enough to faithfully present truth from week to week in our classes. We must also equip our students to discover truth on their own throughout the week. Here are a couple of ways to accomplish this.

1. Teach students to study the Bible inductively.

A number of good resources are available to help students learn to study the Bible in an honest manner. *How To Study The Bible* by G. Raymond Carlson is an example of one of those books and is part of the *Spiritual Discovery Series* produced by *Radiant Life* Curriculum. It is vital that students learn to discover truth on their own, and inductive study is the first step in the process.

2. Teach students to apply what they discover.

The biblical writer James teaches his readers that it is not good enough to know the truth; they must put truth into action in their lives. The Bible is clear that we are held accountable for what we do with the truth we have received. Insist that your students move beyond an academic pursuit while engaged in their quest for truth.

Our society is morally confused. Nearly all of the messages broadcast into our lives tell us that there are no absolute truths. Those who claim to know the truth are labeled as bigots. While this is the case, deep down people know that there is a standard outside of themselves to follow. Christians know what that standard is and must take advantage of every opportunity that God gives to us, faithfully declaring God's truth in love.

IT'S HAPPENING

Tabernaculo Asambleas de Dios located in Bayamon, Puerto Rico, makes the effective presentation of biblical truth a high priority. The church has intentionally created a strategy that has made its Sunday School a primary vehicle for engaging students in the discovery of truths from God's Word.

A key to Tabernaculo Asambleas de Dios' strategy is to have well-prepared teachers who facilitate the discovery of Bible truth. Teachers are trained to be open to innovative teaching methods that make the message of Scripture relevant. Teachers are held account-able to be fully conversant with the material they are teaching. Damaris Cordero, Christian education director for the church, points out that students must have confidence that the teacher knows what he is talking about to avoid the possibility of develop-ing an atmosphere of confusion.

Tabernaculo Asambleas de Dios helps individuals discover biblical truth in a variety of ways. The church offers a variety of study oppor-tunities through its Sunday School program. The leadership of the church recognizes that social and cultural changes in society demand that churches provide learning options. Sister Cordero states, "We have classes that use *Vida* (*Radiant Life*) curriculum; others are taking the Christian Life and Christian Service courses from International Correspondence Institute. Some classes are studying our own curriculum based on the specific needs of segments of our church." One lady who was not regularly attending the church decided to enroll in one of Tabernaculo Asambleas de Dios' special-ized classes. After completing the course on Christian service she testified, "My walk with the Lord has been strengthened with this course, and now I am applying it to my daily life."

The church's commitment to present biblical truth in varied con-texts is seen through their offering of three special education classes for the physically challenged and in their homebound program where teachers go to the homes of members who cannot attend church and present the Sunday School lesson to them. The people of Tabernaculo Asambleas de Dios are currently reaching out to a person who is confined to his home because of legal issues. He is not allowed to leave his house to go to church, so the church goes to him; his family also gathers as the teacher presents the week's lesson. An entire family is being touched because of one church's commitment to spread biblical truth to all who will listen.

Tabernaculo Asambleas de Dios provides a Bible reading club for children. In this program, adults help students get interested in Bible reading and encourage them to read their Bibles at their own pace. Children are provided a coach to help them when they encounter difficult information. An important aspect of the children's Christian education program is Bible memorization. Students not only memorize specific portions of Scripture, they are asked to relate at least three ways the Bible passage applies to their lives or to the lives of others they know.

Tabernaculo Asambleas de Dios encourages students to take Bible learning seriously by offering a library of Christian literature and by offering scholarships to members of their congregation who wish to continue their study of Scripture in the denomination's colleges, institutes, or correspondence schools.

When asked for suggestions that could help other churches focus on the importance of sharing biblical truth with those within their sphere of influence, Sister Cordero offered the following insights. "First of all, study your particular situation and look for your strengths and weaknesses. Identify your weak spots and be willing to make changes. Make learning interesting and exciting." She went on to say, "Get curriculum materials that deal with today's issues and that are compatible with our doctrine. Don't be afraid to spend the necessary funds to get good material and visual aids." Next Cordero emphasized the importance of interactive learning. She pointed out that people learn the Bible best when they participate in the discovery of its truth. Finally, Sister Cordero reminded us that time and effort must be invested in the training of teachers and staff. She cautions us not to forget the spiritual needs of these important components of the Christian education process. Teachers must not only be conveyors of truth, they must also be ongoing consumers as well.

Damaris Cordero concluded her remarks with a quote from her father, "A big Sunday School makes a big and powerful church because people will know in whom they have believed, and they will be firm in their doctrine and in the knowledge of biblical truth." It is obvious that the wisdom of Reverend Doctor Manuel Cordero has not been lost on his daughter.

A FINAL LOOK

Jill navigated her car through noontime traffic. She hated to go downtown at this time of day because it seemed that all the crazies were out. Drivers darted in and out of traffic in their attempt to get back to work before their lunch break expired. Inevitably instead of helping things, these mad dashes caused accidents that slowed the whole process. Unfortunately, an accident occurred ahead of Jill that required her to stop her car.

Jill settled back in her seat and decided to use this time to catch up on the latest political banter. She knew she would be both entertained and informed if she dialed up her favorite national radio talk show. She hit the preset button just in time to hear the host declare that he was the source of all truth. She chuckled at the audacity of such a statement.

As Jill continued to listen to the views of the host, she found herself agreeing with most of what he had to say. It was easy to take such a stance because she came from the same basic school of thought. At points in the presentation, she wondered how anyone could disagree with this man.

Later that afternoon, Jill got back into her car to return home. She had forgotten to turn the radio off earlier in the day and it came to life when she turned on the ignition. She was less familiar with the views of the host of this radio program. She decided to listen to his ideas as she traveled across town. At first she was offended by what she heard. Could he really believe that homosexuality was an acceptable lifestyle? She was tempted to turn off the program, but continued to listen. The arguments he made seemed convincing, but they were so different from what she had been taught throughout her life. The host laughed at those who claimed to have all the truth. He particularly ridiculed those who listened to the radio show host Jill had enjoyed earlier in the day. Although Jill wasn't ready to embrace the latter talk show host's opinions, she began to ask herself, "How do you determine what really is true?"

Jill shook her head as she darted past a slow driver. She thought about people that she had once looked up to who now felt comfortable shaping truth to their liking. It seemed that the whole country was willing to follow the lead of political leaders who could look straight into a television camera and deny things that they knew were true. No longer was this type of action considered a lie; it was simply an altered form of the truth. The postmodern declaration that there is no absolute truth had invaded Jill's world.

As Jill slowed to a stop at the signal light, she wondered when this way of thinking began. Her mind raced back to her school days when she used to go to Sunday School. Her teachers there taught that God made the earth in six days, but then she would go to school and was told that she had evolved from a monkey. She remembered her confusion. In some ways it was a relief that her parents stopped letting her go to Sunday School, but many of the lessons she learned there still influenced the way she interpreted things in her life today.

Jill continued her thinking about this whole issue of truth. Was it as important as she thought or was it relative, as many taught today? She wondered what she was teaching her children. Were they receiving truth? How would she know if she was teaching them correctly if she wasn't even sure that she knew what was true? Jill was startled as the driver in back of her blasted his horn to inform her that the light had turned green.

After Jill recovered from her embarrassment, she returned to her thoughts, continuing on her journey home. She began to think about the green light that had just permitted her to move forward. There was no purple light that meant, "Maybe you can go and maybe you can't." It was pretty simple, red means stop, yellow means get ready to stop, and green means go. Jill wished that there was a simple standard like signal lights for her to live by.

That evening at dinner Jill ambushed her husband by asking him if he thought that there was a single standard of truth. Joe responded with a grunt and asked her for more green beans.

Jill persisted in her pursuit of truth. She shared some of the thoughts that engulfed her throughout the day. She wanted Joe to know that she was serious and needed his help in finding some kind of resolution. Jill started listing some of the things that had provoked her thinking. Is one religion superior to another religion? Is it okay to fabricate things to entertain your children? Are there situations when telling a lie is actually more advantageous than telling the truth? Are there red, yellow, and green lights that can be obeyed that will direct a person's life?

Joe, still trying to recover from the shock of such questions, told Jill that he really didn't know, but he thought that it was extremely important that everybody be tolerant of each other and live according to what they think is correct.

Jill told Joe that she used to think that way but she could no longer accept it. She couldn't see how it could be possible that everybody could be right.

Jill tried to explain her thoughts by referring back to the traffic light illustration. She explained that if each colored light could mean whatever a person wanted it to mean, everyone who pulled up to that light could do whatever they wanted. The result would be a massive pileup. As Jill assessed the world she lived in, it appeared that pileup was already taking place in her society.

Something deep down inside Jill said there had to be a standard for everybody to live by. She just didn't know what that standard was.

As Joe ate the last of his meat loaf, he heard Jill softly whisper, "I have got to find out what that standard is."

 **ENDNOTES**

[1]Barna Research Group, Ltd. (2000). *More than twenty million churched adults actively involved in spiritual growth efforts,* [Online]. Available FTP: www.barna.org
[2]Barna Research Group, Ltd. (1997). *Values,* [Online]. Available FTP: www.barna.org
[3]Ibid.

ADDITIONAL TRAINING MATERIALS

FROM THE
PUBLISHERS OF *RADIANT LIFE* CURRICULUM

Teachers

StepOne for

GPH - 02-0285
ISBN -0-88243-285-0

StepONE
A GUIDE FOR TEACHERS

NURSERY

NEWBORN–AGE 2

How smart are babies?

What can they learn at church?

How can we keep the nursery safe, secure, and happy?

A ministry of Gospel Publishing House

StepONE
A GUIDE FOR TEACHERS

What's normal for this age?

What are they able to learn about God?

How can I get their attention?

EARLY CHILDHOOD

AGES 2 YEARS–KINDERGARTEN

A ministry of Gospel Publishing House

GPH - 02-0286
ISBN -0-88243-286-9

StepONE
A GUIDE FOR TEACHERS

ELEMENTARY

AGES 6-12

How do I minister to the whole child?

Does my room setup matter?

How do I discipline my class?

What about leading children to Christ?

A ministry of Gospel Publishing House

GPH - 02-0287
ISBN -0-88243-287-7

Age-Level
Training Booklets

GPH - 02-0288
ISBN -0-88243-288-5

GPH - 02-0289
ISBN -0-88243-289-3

GPH - 02-0290
ISBN -0-88243-290-7

Here's How
Videos

Early Childhood
GPH - 26-0680

Elementary
GPH - 26-0681

170

Age-Level Training Videos

All 4 Videos
GPH - 26-0684

Youth
GPH - 26-0682

Adult
GPH - 26-0683

Additional Teacher Training Books

GPH - 02-0620
ISBN -0-88243-620-1

GPH - 02-0335
ISBN -0-88243-335-0

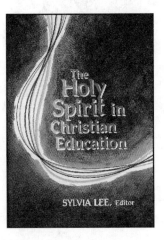

GPH - 02-0854
ISBN -0-88243-854-9

GPH - 02-0664
ISBN -0-88243-664-3

GPH - 02-0327
ISBN -0-88243-327-X

GPH - 02-0798
ISBN -0-88243-798-4

Leadership

Instructors Guides Available

GPH - 02-0698
ISBN -0-88243-698-8

GPH - 02-0655
ISBN -0-88243-655-4

Training Books

GPH - 02-0699
ISBN -0-88243-699-6

Building *the* **Winning Team**

MOVING ON TO MATURITY

ALTON GARRISON

Getting Into *the* **Game**

TEACHING TOWARD INVOLVEMENT

EDITED BY LARRY THOMAS

GPH - 02-0324
ISBN -0-88243-324-5

Playing *Your* **Position**

INVESTING YOURSELF IN OTHERS

COMPILED BY
LARRY THOMAS

GPH - 02-4101
ISBN -0-88243-410-1

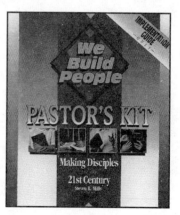

We Build People

PASTOR'S KIT

Making Disciples
for the
21st Century
Steven R. Mills

GPH - 26-0692

More
Age-Level Training Books

GPH - 02-0404
ISBN -0-88243-404-7

GPH - 02-0405
ISBN -0-88243-405-5

 GPH - 02-0408
ISBN -0-88243-408-X

GPH - 02-0406
ISBN -0-88243-406-3

GPH - 02-0407
ISBN -0-88243-407-1